D1064075

Green *in* Gridlock

CONSERVATION LEADERSHIP SERIES

Sponsored by

THE MEADOWS CENTER
FOR WATER AND THE ENVIRONMENT
TEXAS STATE UNIVERSITY

Andrew Sansom, General Editor

A list of other titles in this series
may be found at the back of the book.

Green *in* Gridlock

COMMON GOALS, COMMON GROUND, AND COMPROMISE

Paul Walden Hansen

FOREWORD BY ANDREW SANSOM

Texas A&M University Press
College Station

This paper meets the requirements of ANSI/NISO Z39.48-1992
(Permanence of Paper).
Binding materials have been chosen for durability.

Parts of chapter 1, "Green in Gridlock," first appeared in an op-ed published by the
Washington Post on March 15, 2006. Parts of chapter 6, "The Conservation of
Business," appeared in *Directors and Boards* magazine in 2004. Parts of chapters
8 and 13, "Natural Allies" and "Seeing the Fiscal Forest through the Trees," were
syndicated by the *High Country News* in "Writers on the Range." Part of chapters 4
and 12, "Population" and "Echoes from Dinosaur," appeared in *Outdoor America,* the
official magazine of the Izaak Walton League of America. Used by permission; all
other rights reserved.

Library of Congress Cataloging-in-Publication Data

Hansen, Paul, 1952–
    Green in gridlock : common goals, common ground, and compromise / Paul
Walden Hansen ; foreword by Andrew Sansom. — 1st ed.
        p. cm. — (Conservation leadership series)
    Includes bibliographical references and index.
    ISBN-13: 978-1-62349-014-0 (cloth : alk. paper)
    ISBN-10: 1-62349-014-6 (cloth)
    ISBN-13: 978-1-62349-046-1 (e-book)
    ISBN-10: 1-62349-046-4 (e-book)
    1. Conservation of natural resources—Government policy—United States—
History. 2. Conservation of natural resources—Law and legislation—United States—
History. 3. Green movement—United States—History. 4. Conservation leadership—
United States—History. I. Title. II. Series: Conservation leadership series.
    S930. H36 2013
    339.4'9—dc23

                                2013001477

To Luke's generation,
with the hope and faith that you will do better than we did

Contents

Foreword by Andrew Sansom   ix

Acknowledgments   xiii

Introduction   1

1. Green in Gridlock: Addressing the Stalemate   11

2. The Progress Point: The Source of Conservation Success   15

3. The Conservation of Hope: The Ozone Hole, Acid Rain, and Climate Change   27

4. Population: The Fundamental Issue   43

5. Green and God: The Environment of Faith   46

6. The Conservation of Business: Power for Change   50

7. The War in the Woods: Tough Love between Tree Huggers and Timber Beasts   60

8. Natural Allies: Environmentalists, Hunters and Anglers, and Rural Residents   75

9. The Minnesota Miracles: Real Success through Engagement   103

10. Land Conservation: Messaging for Success   114

11. Eating Their Own Young: The Nader Nadir   121

12. Echoes from Dinosaur: The Perils of Compromise   128

13. Seeing the Fiscal Forest through the Trees:
    Conservation Spending and the National Debt   135

14. Rules of Engagement: Making Collaboration Real   140

15. Infinite Harm: If We Fail   147

16. The Ten Convenient Truths of Conservation Success   152

Additional Reading   161

Index   165

Foreword

ONE OF THE WORST FIGHTS I EVER GOT INTO as executive director of the Texas Parks and Wildlife Department was over a proposal to add an additional nine holes to the historic golf course at Bastrop State Park near Austin, Texas. The old course had a loyal following of largely Hispanic golfers whose children had learned to play there, and several of them had become skilled enough at the game to be awarded scholarships to compete at the college level, an educational opportunity that otherwise may not have been available to them. At the same time, this park happens to contain habitat for the endangered Houston Toad, and the proposed additions would have impacted some of that habitat. As a result, the project became the subject of a pitched battle between environmental interests that adamantly opposed any addition to the golf course and the community for whom it had become over the years so important. To complicate things further, the local state representative at the time, who favored the proposal, was the leading supporter of conservation in the Texas Legislature and the sponsor of critical legislation to provide funding for parks across the state, including Bastrop. Although the additional nine holes were ultimately built, the dispute caused permanent damage to the credibility and effectiveness of some of the environmental participants, and some bitterness from the episode lingers to this day.

In this third title in the Conservation Leadership Series sponsored by the Meadows Center for Water and the Environment at Texas State University, Paul Hansen, the former head of the Izaak Walton League, one of America's earliest and most effective conservation organizations, describes real-life experiences like the Bastrop golf course fight to demonstrate how in the presence (or absence) of open-mindedness, pragmatism, and patience alliances are formed (or avoided), leadership is rewarded (or denied), compromise is reached (or abandoned), and progress is made (or thwarted).

Throughout the history of conservation, there have been a handful of books that changed how we think and brought us to an entirely new level of awareness and success in how we manage, protect, and use our natural heritage. This book does that for our time. Hansen's insights have never been more critical to the conservation movement than they are today, when the level of polarization in public life seems higher than ever and unwillingness to compromise is all too often touted as a virtue. This unfortunate circumstance is reflected in contemporary polls which demonstrate that while Americans do care about the environment, they are often unsure of environmentalists, who sometimes seem to prefer fighting to winning.

In these pages, Paul Hansen taps into his years of experience and offers practical lessons for all sides on how to join forces, how to negotiate and accept incremental successes, and how to purposefully make progress toward what the American people solidly favor: sound conservation of our natural resources and protection of the environment.

Today, through the determined work of those who finally heard the message in this book, and with the leadership of the legislator who was responsive to his community, several thousand acres of Houston Toad habitat have been added to Bastrop State Park, more than tripling its size; the old golf course has been expanded to eighteen holes; and all the sales taxes on sporting goods in Texas are dedicated to the support of parks at both the state and local levels. Paul Hansen would have approved.

—Andrew Sansom
General Editor, Conservation Leadership Series

Acknowledgments

ONE OF THE REWARDING PARTS of engaging in such a speculative effort as writing your first book is the chance to thank in writing the people who have helped so much along the way. My parents, the late Carl and Phyllis Hansen, put such a strong emphasis on work and education and gave me so much. My best friends of forty years, Lisa Neff and Ken Olson, are listeners and advisors for life. My college advisor, the late Robert Bieri, was mentor to Harvard paleontologist Steven Jay Gould and a host of us others. Erik Thuesen, Bieri's closest protégé, relentlessly encouraged this project. The late Jack Lorenz, Izaak Walton League of America (IWLA) executive director, mentored so many of us. Maitland Sharpe's wisdom and influence flows throughout the book. Pat Noonan, John Turner, and Jon Roush have shown leadership that has been followed by so many of us—providing the intellectual framework for bringing people together from different directions for positive conservation outcomes. Canadian members of Parliament John Fraser and the late Stan Darling, along with fellow Canadians Michael Perley, Adele Hurley, George Rejhon, Ray Robinson, and Janice Hilchie worked tirelessly for years to successfully give North America relief from acid rain pollution. Rollin Sparrowe set a standard for sensible and inclusive wildlife management leadership that may never be matched. Former Louisiana Pacific CEO Mark Suwyn showed the vision and risk tolerance to put an untested conservationist on a large public company board. LP executive leaders Rick Frost and Curt Stevens, as well as board leaders Archie Dunham and Gary Cook, gave me the extra time and attention needed to make having a nonprofit leader a successful part of a public company board. Denis Hayes and Jack Ward Thomas encouraged me to take the career risk that came with agreeing to serve on LP's board. Henson Moore and Steve Lovett took on the challenge of raising the environmental performance of an entire industry.

As IWLA Midwest office director and associate executive director, Bill Grant was my right hand and partner on many difficult conservation issues and situations for fifteen years. His grace and competence was key to many of the Minnesota miracles and still is in his new role as the state's chief energy officer. There are too many Izaak Walton League volunteer leaders to mention, but a few stand out: Charlie and Leila Wiles, David and Margo Zentner, Bill and Carol West, Tim and Pat Reid, Mike Chenoweth, Jim Haring, the late Stanford Adams, and the late Donald Ferris—an American hero at Iwo Jima and in conservation defense of the homeland. There is a host of Izaak Walton League staff who worked in great good faith with me and each other for so many years: Mike Lynch, Anne MacGlashan, Mary Rubin, Miguel Carvallo, Tom Franklin, Debbie Chopas, Jon Birdsong, Nancy Lange, Tom Sadler, Mike Higgs, Fran Raymond Price, Ione Mansfield, Casey Williams, Earl Hower, Jason McGarvey,

Jay Clark, Cathy Berger, Kevin Proescholdt, and Audrey Morris—to name a few. For years, I participated in efforts with environmental leaders in the "Green Group" who struggled to be cooperators on mission while being competitors for members, money, and media. Our deftly gifted coordinator Julie Waterman guided so many of our efforts. Though we could not always agree on strategy, Bill Meadows, Rodger Schlickheisen, Fred Krupp, Carl Pope, John Adams, Rebecca Wodder, Will Rogers, Bob Musil, Bud Ris, John Flicker, Gene Karpinski, Brent Blackwelder, Paul Gorman, and Francis Beinecke all came to the table wanting the best environmental outcome for the nation and the world. It was a joy watching Jean Hocker and then Rand Wentworth build the land trust movement from almost nothing to the nation's largest cooperative land protection venture. Ralph Grossi did much the same with the American Farmland Trust. The late Jim Range gave us the Theodore Roosevelt Conservation Partnership and a legacy of friendship and professional profanity that will not be equaled soon. Col. Don Sowold, formerly of the National Guard, and Col. Jim Corbin, formerly of the US Army Corps of Engineers, showed what could be done when individuals in large and often bureaucratic organizations reach out to stakeholders. Bob Model gives credit to others, but he more than anyone started the American Wildlife Conservation Partners, a collaboration of the hunting conservation organizations. If they can focus on conservation policy rather than conservative politics, they will enhance wildlife conservation for years to come. Jackson Hole friends Charlie Thompson, Jim Nokes, Steve Sharkey, Luther Propst, and Liz Storer all commented on many concepts and early drafts.

Andy Sansom's career mirrors the theme of this book. He has worked with the broadest spectrum of Americans and accomplished great conservation success. He and Texas A&M University Press's Conservation Leadership Series provided the perfect organization for publishing this work. They have, in Shannon Davies, the only university press editor focused solely on the natural environment. From the beginning, Shannon showed great understanding of the environmental field in general and this project in particular. When she wrote me that this book "will resonate with others who, like me, find themselves wondering why the concerns we actually share in this country can't, somehow, actually be shared," I knew that TAMU Press had to be the publisher.

After my twenty-five years with the Izaak Walton League, much of what appears here is based on themes I worked on and learning I experienced with that organization. Content on the Greater Yellowstone area was acquired during my time with the Nature Conservancy. Content on forestry, population, faith, park policy, and wildlife management funding all have roots in work I did for the Izaak Walton League, including some special reports and articles for their magazine *Outdoor America*.

Finally, I want to thank my father-in-law, Jim Stratman, for his constant encouragement that the project "would unfold" and my brothers-in-law, Steve and Mark Stratman, for their advice on all things computer, printing, and publishing. Of course, most of all, thank you, Kay, for all your support and Lad Labrador for getting me away from the desk at the end of the day and on to the trail.

Despite all this help, I alone am responsible for what appears here.

Green in Gridlock

Introduction

Insanity: doing the same thing over and
over again and expecting different results.
—Albert Einstein

The need is not really for more brains, the need is now for a gentler,
a more tolerant people than those who won for us against the ice, the tiger,
and the bear. The hand that hefted the ax, out of some old blind allegiance
to the past, fondles the machine gun as lovingly. It is a habit that man
will have to break to survive, but the roots go very deep.
—Loren Eiseley, *The Immense Journey*

EARLY IN MY CAREER, after one of my young-person rants, an older and more experienced conservationist asked me, "Paul do you want to make a point or make progress?" The question became a driving motivator for me during three decades in conservation leadership.

I want progress. I want success.

Ask any environmentalist, and they will tell you that we need to do much more to protect the Earth and that there is a great deal of independent science to support that view. Ask what the solutions are, and the answer gets shorter. Ask what is the most effective strategy for implementing those solutions and you might not get any answer at all.

Most of us in conservation are much better at describing problems than we are at presenting solutions. Even if we know what needs to be done, and can describe solutions, we clearly have an even more difficult

1

time figuring out how to get these solutions implemented. We see this in the fact that most national environmental progress has ground to a halt and is stuck in gridlock—especially since 1990. The new generation of business, faith, political, environmental, and other leaders must do better than we have done. We are running out of the gift of time.

Today, support for a greener society is high among all age groups but is highest among youth of all races and classes than it is for their elders. In this book, I hope to convince this new generation not to make the same mistakes that have kept previous generations from success.

The question is no longer whether we should take care of the environment; it is how do we accomplish it? Most often, progress requires a choice: either civil engagement with each other to identify our common ground and implement compromise solutions or failure. My generation has proved that. When we have succeeded, our success was based on making the first choice.

We have not succeeded often enough. Environmental protection has not progressed to the extent necessary to protect the most vulnerable people and places on our planet. Success requires the broader support that comes from a more inclusive and collaborative approach that accepts compromise as an essential building block to progress. Going forward, conservation cannot succeed from a confrontational or insular base of advocates.

Adversarial advocacy is not working, and radical environmentalism has now become part of the problem. Too often, much of traditional environmentalism is based on holier than thou affirmations of our own tribe's moral superiority and political correctness. We need to find the cross-cultural willpower, guts, and humility to connect with others and find where our interests overlap to a point where we can get started taking action. "All or nothing" rarely results in all and often results in nothing.

Imagine if people with different perspectives came to the table to engage honestly with each other, listen, build trust, and find common ground. Imagine the progress that could be made by such an approach, rather than the strident self-serving gridlock we find ourselves in today. Imagine our society with a can-do attitude toward conservation innovation—a place where limiting waste and inefficiency is taken seriously, and the best technology is put to work in ways that renew and nourish our nation's environment and economy. Imagine a country where positive investments in the future and a balanced approach to environmental protection are valued to assure true long-term prosperity and financial security for present and future generations.

There are many great books that describe the breadth and depth of the environmental issues challenging humankind. Other authors have described in detail and with great skill the collapse of other civilizations, extinction of magnificent species, loss of open space and habitat, decline of the blue oceans, degradation of plant communities and wildlife populations worldwide, impacts of toxins, reductions in topsoil and arable land, pollution of air and water, and the more prosaic but most profound of all—the loss of microscopic organisms essential to recycling nutrients and restoring biogeochemical cycles on which all life depends. There are many others who have written eloquent exhortations imploring us all to do something about all of this. Still others have done a beautiful and poetic job celebrating the beauty of the natural world, often with splendid photos and art in large-format publications or audio-video presentations.

This book is focused on progress: examining how it has occurred in the past and how we can ensure it will occur more often in the future. When it comes to environmental conservation, it is progress alone that matters. We need to go beyond exhortations to the already converted, as songs sung to the choir. Even the most eloquent appeals are now adding little to durable progress. People are numbed by the litany of descriptions of what is being lost, and the palliative of beautiful coffee table nature books now only increases the pain. Success depends on moving from repetitive problem identification to solution implementation, yet most environmentalists are much better at describing the crisis than the solution. People want to know what to do and how to get started.

This will require supporting leaders ready for honest engagement and problem solving. Demonizing others will not cure a problem or find a durable solution. Almost half of our society now self-identify as moderate, pragmatic, and politically independent—this book is especially for you. You are our real progress leaders. The real world is not black or white. It is filled with subtlety and nuance. Grey is the color of truth. The wing nuts with their anger and fatuous sound bites get the media, but the pragmatic centrists have the numbers and the solutions. Those of us who want progress need to see those who demonize, on both sides, for what they really are—advocates for human failure and environmental catastrophe.

In the pages that follow, we will examine environmental success— what has worked to successfully address a number of the most vital conservation issues ever faced. We will see how diverse groups of people have made fantastic progress, oftentimes dramatically and against great odds, on critical environmental issues. We will also look at what has not worked and at opportunities for progress that remain available. We will explore ways to engage with others so we can get past the gridlock that has hampered progress on environmental conservation, and so many other key issues, over the last couple of decades. We will see the value of a new commitment to the innovative, can-do spirit that best aligns with success—giving specific examples of issues where we could make immediate progress through this approach.

People prefer pragmatism to partisanship, because it works. With the innate wisdom that is key to human success, most Americans are rejecting insular institutions, the "gotcha" politics of no, and tactics of personal destruction that infect our society and our institutions. Never before has the public shown more distrust for our own leaders and dismay at their inability to make progress. Never before have political parties been so unpopular, with approval ratings nearing single digits. While the country is moving toward the center, where things get done, the two political parties are being driven to their activist wings. The Congress itself seems frustrated, and one of the few things they agree on is that the institution is broken. When Sen. Chris Dodd, Democrat from Connecticut, retired he called the political system "completely dysfunctional." Republican Minority Leader Mitch McConnell called Dodd's speech "one of the most important in the history of the Senate." Still, neither side seems to be able to break through the self-destruction that grips the government. In this divisive scenario, they cannot solve problems on widely popular issues such as conservation, where there is majority support building from the center.

There are practical examples of success and solutions for success on some of our most challenging conservation issues. We should recognize that most people are intelligent, rational, hardworking people of good will. As management guru Peter Drucker taught us, if we struggle with each other it is usually because of mistrust, outdated ideas, a narrow conception of problems, or internal misunderstandings. Many methods and technical fixes are available but remain underutilized. Too many powerful solutions continue to languish behind public indifference, political squabbling, bipartisan gridlock, or end-game debates.

My bias, up front, is that I believe the world faces a severe environment crisis that is already causing enormous suffering in both human and wildlife worlds, particularly among the most vulnerable people and the most specialized species. Recent polling shows that a solid majority of Americans share this view. This is a crisis that will only get much worse unless we use the powerful solutions and processes available that can go a long way to alleviate, if not solve, most of these problems. We need to put them to work, and, too often, we have not. We need to get started. All too frequently, we have let the perfect, as we individually define it, become the enemy of the good.

Yesterday's strategies and tactics will not solve today's environmental challenges. Environmental awareness has increased greatly during my forty-year tour of duty in conservation, but, in most cases, progress has ground to a halt. The public support is there. For decades, we have seen remarkably high polling numbers and other indications of widespread support, if not highest-priority support, for environmental conservation. When conservation is based on the engagement of a diversity of interests and good faith compromise, great progress is made. We might be able to stop bad ideas with harsh tactics, but to build something positive and lasting we must work together.

Radical environmentalism, even if well intended, is usually anti-environmental in outcome. Strident tactics rarely produce durable change and can result in deterrence to overall long-term environmental progress. Natural allies become alienated, even on issues where they might agree. The same message that brings attention to an issue is usually not the message required for solving it. Today, many more Americans call themselves conservationists than environmentalists. Right or wrong, environmentalism has become associated with stridency, which impairs progress.

In the spring of 1972, I spent a week in the Greene County, Ohio, jail with 180 other Antioch College students, local Quakers, and Yellow Springs, Ohio, townspeople. That morning we had quietly and respectfully sat in front of the gates of the Wright Patterson Air Force base to protest the continuing war in Vietnam and its expansion into Cambodia. I meant no disrespect to those who made a different choice and served, and I honor their sacrifice to this day. In fact, quite a number of veterans joined us that morning in our respectful civil disobedience. Like many Americans, after years of watching the carnage, we had become convinced the war was wrong. After our brief and well-fed incarceration—with our meals provided by Sheriff Russ Bradley's wife, to whom we sent flowers after being released—we returned to campus as minor heroes feeling pretty good about ourselves. I now view this as an awful mistake.

Today, I am convinced that our action and the actions of other protestors prolonged the war, the death, and the suffering. We could have done much better. We took what was rapidly becoming mainstream awareness of our nation's mistaken involvement in Vietnam and made it a counterculture cause. By misidentifying opposition to the war in Vietnam with alternative culture, we made it harder, not easier, for a majority of the US public to identify with the issue and support an end to the conflict. This realization has haunted me for years. What if we had carefully made our case with the public, developing thoughtful messages, strategically targeting swing members of Congress, politely engaging with their constituents, and respectfully organizing support in their districts? How much sooner would our leaders have ended the quagmire and suffering? How many lives would we have saved?

Today, after forty years in conservation, I have similar questions about the failure of much environmental strategy to reach the solid majority of people who support environmental protection. Most Americans get it. They understand that there are significant environmental problems, and maybe even an ecological disaster unfolding on the planet. There is little doubt that most of this problem is caused by just one species—humans—and that it deserves a war-level mobilization effort to remedy. They know that both Republicans and Democrats have mortgaged America's future with reckless tax cuts, wasteful earmarks, uncontrolled spending, and deceptive accounting whereby some items are somehow "off budget." According to Adm. Mike Mullen, former chair of the Joint Chiefs of Staff, this threatens our nation as much as any foreign adversary. Similarly, by failing to make high-return investments in nature, we know that our leaders have also amassed a conservation debt that must be paid. We care deeply about the future. We understand these problems. We need to do more to solve them.

Under the best conditions, environmental issues are the type of problems that are hard for the human species to deal with. Most often, the impacts accrue slowly over time before they become serious or tragic. Even when our own lives are at stake, we are not hardwired to deal well with silent, slow-motion, and long-term crises. Ask any doctor—as a species we do not deal well with events that are not directly visible but build up incrementally with eventually catastrophic results. As I get older, I am personally reminded of this at each annual physical. As with personal health, however, there is also no doubt that we really can do a great deal to improve our environment—if we can commit ourselves to addressing issues more constructively and together.

Similarly, humans do not attach as much importance to "malignant" problems as distinct from "malevolent" ones driven by an evil-intentioned adversary. Each year, over ten times as many people die in traffic accidents than died during the September 11, 2001, attacks. Drunk and distracted driving is epidemic, but we do not spend a fraction of the money cracking down on highway safety that we spend on terrorist threats. Some credible estimates put premature death from environmental contaminants at twice the level of highway fatalities. We have a propensity to sidestep malignant problems, such as environmental ones, while focusing primarily on malevolent ones—even if the objective risk for loss of life is less. According to many scholars, sea-level rise due to climate is the big global issue that could cause "the end of civilization as we know it," but how many of us give it as much attention as we do the price of a gallon of gasoline?

For decades, public opinion polls have shown unequivocally that most people care about the environment but are unsure about environmentalists. While they might trust environmentalists to identify problems, they do not trust them to solve problems. Business and government fare even worse in public opinion on conservation. Almost everyone agrees that we have a moral duty to leave the earth in as good or better shape for our children and their children, but they do not respond well to doom and gloom rhetoric. Over the years, we have depressed and demoralized people and scared our children with a litany of despair over the environmental problems we face. This litany tells only half the story. There are very serious conservation issues, such as climate change, we must confront. However, for this and most other environmental problems, there are equal and compelling solutions that are cost-effective in traditional economic terms. This is especially true if we do our cost accounting honestly—if we truly consider the very real costs of inaction.

I have been blessed with a conservation career that put me in the room with more diverse groups than anyone else I know. Back in the 1970s, I was a conservation volunteer promoting the Alaska Lands Act for six years, spending two summer field seasons in that awesome place. I spent nine years as a consultant for the Canadian government working to reduce trans-boundary acid rain pollution. I spent twenty-eight years working for nonprofit conservation groups. For twenty-five years, I was with one of the smallest but oldest national groups, the very politically diverse Izaak Walton League of America—with twelve years as their executive director. I was Greater Yellowstone program director for the Nature Conservancy, the world's largest conservation organization.

During those years, I worked with many of America's top leaders in government, environmental organizations, sportsmen groups, citizen leaders, innovative businesses, and trade associations. I chaired the Green Group, the leadership forum of the large national environmental organizations, and was a founder of the American Wildlife Conservation Partners, the leadership forum of hunting conservation leaders. For over a decade, I was the only person who was part of both of these groups of outdoor lovers, who do not spend enough time talking to each other and finding ways to work together. I spent almost nine years on the board of a Fortune 500 company and worked to help an entire forest products industry to improve its environmental performance and motivate its poor performers to a higher standard. I attended at least twenty-five meetings in the White House and hundreds in the Congress. I was a guest at least five hundred times at small conservation clubs and meetings throughout rural America, where I saw plenty of wisdom and dedication from extraordinary "ordinary" Americans giving their personal time and energy to make the world a better place by conserving outdoor America.

Through it all, I learned much from this great diversity of people: sportsmen, politicians, environmentalists, legislators, reporters, business leaders, clergy, and many ordinary citizens in communities throughout the United States and Canada. I have found overwhelming common ground on the need to conserve environmental and natural resources and a desire to take that common ground and use it to begin to make progress at a scale and pace equal to the challenge before us. I have seen great success come from honest engagement and cooperation and give several powerful accounts of this success.

We are, quite literally, all in this together. No one will be able to permanently leave the planet anytime soon. If we want to succeed in protecting this place, we need to start acting that way. We need to bring some kindness and a measure of humility to our cause. With blunt idealism, and a policy of engagement that starts with first steps and a common-ground approach to cost-effective environmental conservation, we might just save the world and have some fun doing it.

Green in Gridlock

Addressing the Stalemate

Ideological and partisan rivals do have something in common—an
exaggerated sense of their own righteousness, aggravated by an inability to
recognize that the other side may not be evil incarnate with nothing to offer.
—Colbert I. King, *Washington Post*

I have come to recognize some of the signs of the madness that leads to
tragedies on a grand scale. Old grievances are resurrected and refurbished with
a new intensity. Ancient injustices are insufferably aggravated. Politics are
elevated to religion. Religion is mired in politics. It is different every time. Yet it
always starts the same way: with a loss of civility, tolerance and reason.
—Holocaust survivor Joe Schlesinger, journalist, author, and former
Canadian Broadcasting Corporation foreign correspondent

ENVIRONMENTAL CONSERVATION is not a conservative or liberal
cause. It is certainly not a countercultural cause. It is everyone's
cause. It is an issue that is embraced by most humans, but one where
essential progress has been hard to come by for decades.

It has been a constant in public opinion polls that an overwhelming percentage of Americans favor sound conservation of natural resources and the environment. Overwhelming majorities of Americans of all political persuasions believe that "conserving the country's
natural resources—land, air and water—is patriotic." Four out of five
Americans agreed with this statement and believe we can protect land
and water and have a strong economy at the same time. Other nations
have found similar results. This includes strong majorities across all
major demographic categories: ethnic, religious, racial, age, gender, and

political party affiliation. Few issues enjoy this broad diversity of public support.

So why is it so difficult to make progress on an issue that is this popular? Why has the environmental debate become almost hysterically polarized?

There are a variety of theories on why such a well-accepted cause faces such insurmountable gridlock. In the United States, these include corporate shortsightedness, the influence of money on the legislative process, the alleged interest of Democrats in having the environment as a perennial campaign issue, and the perceived antipathy of many Republican leaders. Many of today's leaders, from both parties, seem out of step with the US public when it comes to responsible environmental conservation. Americans do not want rhetoric—they want solutions. These are increasingly scarce, especially at the national level.

The rabid opposition of the far right to environmental progress is now a fixture and a radical break with the history and tradition of the party of Theodore Roosevelt and the fundamental progress of the Richard Nixon–Gerald Ford years. Ironically, the tactics of some environmentalists also play a major role in creating political polarization and gridlock on environmental policy. Given the widespread but latent support of a strong majority of Americans in favor of environmental conservation, the inability of some environmental proponents to think and act strategically comprises a major obstacle to progress. As Sen. Evan Bayh, a Democrat from Indiana, said when he announced his retirement, "too many people would rather have nothing than half a loaf." History shows us that environmental progress always comes in half loaves. Pres. Lyndon Johnson said, "Any person not willing to settle for half a loaf has never been hungry." By insisting on full-loaf solutions, we are simply creating an environmental gridlock in the United States that does not allow for progress.

Conservation is itself a neighborly vision; it asks how we can live together without hurting each other. It asks us to consider the long-

term consequences of our actions and the effect on future generations of humans and the other species with which we share the planet.
As with the federal deficit, Americans understand this central issue
of conservation. It is about the prevention of problems at lower cost
before they become much worse. We pay now, we pay more later, or
our children pay *much* more later. What many people do not always
recognize, however, is how cost-effective environmental measures can
be. Most Americans share the widely held goals of clean air, water,
and a reasonable legacy of open space and wildlife habitat. We aspire
to have the next generation do better than we did, but many of us fear
they will be the first generation not to do better than their parents. It
does not have to be that way. The technical solutions are there, but our
society needs to begin to implement them widely.

Too often, we are offered the simplistic palliative of individual action as a solution to environmental problems. Leading by example and
showing what is possible is a good thing, but it cannot be a substitute
for collective action. When individual action gives people the sense
they are doing something effective and therefore do not need to support societal action, it can be counterproductive. A level playing field
of sensible regulations is essential to national and international environmental progress. Voluntary action by a few cannot save the planet.

Today, traditional environmental strategies and tactics do not provide solutions at a pace or scale that is needed. While most Americans
are generally comfortable with environmentalists' goals, they are much
less comfortable with their tactics and rhetoric. The doom and gloom
pronouncements that identified problems and attracted people's attention in the 1970s is old and worn out. It now depresses and demoral-
izes people. Worse, it makes them feel guilty rather than excited about
the opportunities and prospects for progress. Hope motivates better
than fear.

The activist approach that identified issues back in the 1970s will
not work today. In fact, on many issues it may be the opposite of the

mutual engagement that is now needed. We now have a couple of decades of proof that yesterday's tactics do not work. The answer is not to push harder in the same direction but to utilize new approaches. Back in the 1970s, environmental awareness was relatively low and conservation was a concern of only a minority of Americans. Today, with strong majorities in favor of conservation, the issue requires a can-do message that emphasizes our common ground, not our differences. Minority causes need to emphasize what distinguishes them. Majority causes need to emphasize the positive values we share.

Sulfate ion wet deposition, 1994

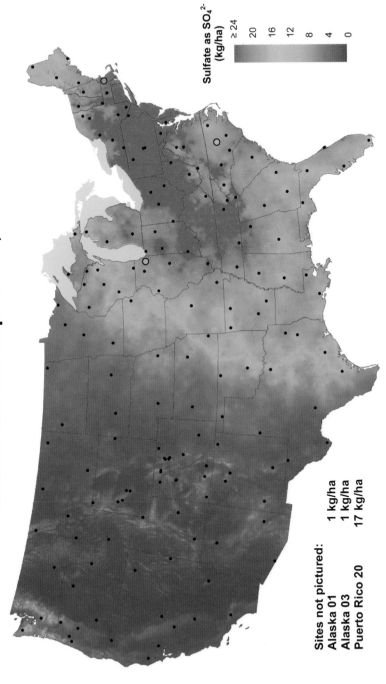

Sulfate as SO₄²⁻ (kg/ha)

≥ 24
20
16
12
8
4
0

Sites not pictured:
Alaska 01   1 kg/ha
Alaska 03   1 kg/ha
Puerto Rico 20   17 kg/ha

National Atmospheric Deposition Program/National Trends Network
http://nadp.isws.illinois.edu

Acid deposition in 1994 and 2010. These pollution reductions saved eight dollars for every one dollar in cost. *Source:* National Atmospheric Deposition Program/National Trends Network (nadp.isws.illinois.edu)

Sulfate ion wet deposition, 2010

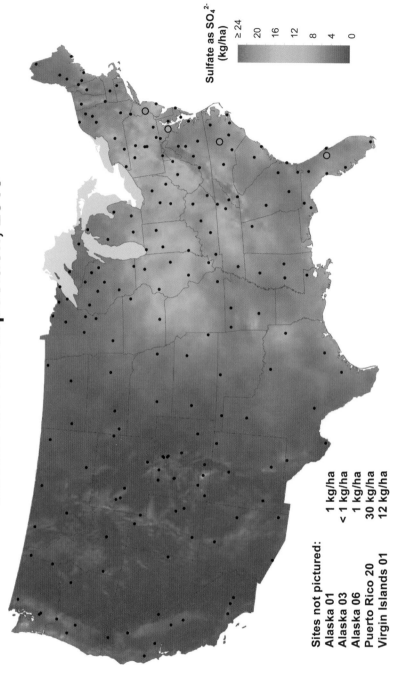

Sulfate as SO₄²⁻ (kg/ha)

≥24
20
16
12
8
4
0

Sites not pictured:

Alaska 01	1 kg/ha
Alaska 03	<1 kg/ha
Alaska 06	1 kg/ha
Puerto Rico 20	30 kg/ha
Virgin Islands 01	12 kg/ha

National Atmospheric Deposition Program/National Trends Network
http://nadp.isws.illinois.edu

Acid deposition in 1994 and 2010. These pollution reductions saved eight dollars for every one dollar in cost. *Source*: National Atmospheric Deposition Program/National Trends Network (nadp.isws.illinois.edu)

2
The Progress Point
The Source of Conservation Success

Activism is admirable, necessary and self-undermining—
the more passionate, the more self-blinding.
—David Brooks, *New York Times*

Paul, do you want to make a point or make progress?
—David Hawkins, Natural Resources Defense Council

Too OFTEN, IT SEEMS that many environmentalists would rather fight than win. Taking strong positions becomes more important than taking effective ones. We spend too much time talking to each other or, worse, fighting among ourselves on the finer but less relevant details of the solutions we propose. Not nearly enough time is spent reaching outside our groups to others—and listening. Environmentalists have especially failed to reach businesses, political moderates, and rural Americans who live closest to nature—the very people who are the most key to success. There is a reason for this. When environmental leaders do try to engage or support a smart and strategic compromise, they risk being publicly condemned as too soft or too compromising. It is a smear that can be deadly to a career.

Conservation is a righteous issue, but strident or self-righteous behavior is not the way to gather the broad support needed for success. Nothing dissuades people like righteousness, and some parts of the environmental community are cursed by it. Thinking and acting ideologically rather than strategically works against success in protecting ecosystems, wildlife, and human health. Opportunities for important alliances, partnerships, and durable conservation gains are lost. An inconvenient truth of environmental progress is that virtually every major gain in conservation over the last one hundred years is the result of a bipartisan compromise. When incremental progress becomes unacceptable, it results in a stalemate and stops progress on most conservation issues.

We can see how this dynamic has played out with most of our fundamental legal infrastructure for providing environmental protection nationwide. For example, in the 1970s, when people worked together, we passed an amazing array of environmental legislation that established a legal framework for the environment. A new agency—the Environmental Protection Agency (EPA)—was established to oversee the administration of many of these sweeping new laws. These include the National Environmental Policy Act of 1970, Clean Air Act of 1970, Federal Advisory Committee Act of 1972, Federal Water Pollution Control Act of 1972, Marine Mammal Protection Act of 1972, Endangered Species Act of 1973, Forest and Rangeland Renewable Resources Planning Act of 1974, National Forest Management Act of 1976, Federal Land Management and Policy Act of 1976, and the Toxic Substance Control Act of 1976. Republican Presidents Richard Nixon and Gerald Ford signed all of these acts of Congress into law, if sometimes reluctantly.

During the 1990s, most of these major laws governing the fundamental environmental infrastructure of our nation, including the Clean Air Act, the Clean Water Act, the Endangered Species Act, the Resource Conservation and Recovery Act, and the Comprehensive Environmental Response, Compensation and Liability Act (Superfund), were due to be reauthorized. All had been reauthorized before, some several times, during both Republican and Democratic presidencies. We took the lessons learned and improved the law. However, since 1990, none of these fundamental pieces of environmental law has been reauthorized, not one—crippling progress in each area. By not updating existing statutes, two decades of learning, science, and experience have not been incorporated into the law.

During that time, progress nearly halted on emerging issues, such as climate change—which threatens the entire planet—and on old ones, such as improving overall energy efficiency, which saves money, prevents pollution, and reduces dependence on foreign oil. The Environmental Protection Agency tells us that 860 billion gallons of raw sewage still flow into our waterways annually. And while our air is cleaner, it is still not healthy for at least one hundred million Americans—not only in cities but some rural areas as well.

The nation's most protective public land conservation law, the Wilderness Act of 1964, was a major compromise. It protected only nine million acres—a small fraction of the land that qualified as most pristine. But it did set up an inclusive and deliberate process for adding the highest level of protection to more areas of federal public lands. Every president in the years since the act was passed has signed legislation adding to the wilderness preservation system. Pres. Ronald Reagan signed the most acres into law. By 2010, the national wilderness preservation system included almost 110 million acres. Few environmentalists would argue that passing the Wilderness Act was a bad idea—but would they support this compromise if it were before them today?

In 1970, Congress passed the Clean Air Act with overwhelming nonpartisan agreement: 73 to 0 in the Senate and 374 to 1 in the House. The 1973 Endangered Species Act passed in the Senate 92 to 0 and 355 to 4 in the House. The National Environmental Protection Act of 1970 passed the Senate unanimously and the House 372–15. The Clean

Water Act (1972) passed 52–12 in the Senate and 347–23 in the House. Within a decade of passage, all of these laws were reauthorized, some more than once, most by solid majorities. We took learning and experience and refined the law.

Since 1990, reauthorization of all these basic environmental statutes, and many others, were casualties of gridlock. The last time any major federal environmental infrastructure legislation was passed was in 1990 when Pres. George H. W. Bush brokered a compromise, and the Clean Air Act was reauthorized. The act reduced acid rain emissions by ten million tons per year—a 40 percent reduction. This was not the environmental groups' preferred sixteen-million-ton goal, the 60 percent reduction that many scientists told us was needed to protect sensitive ecosystems. It did little to control toxic mercury emissions and did not do enough to clean air in our cities. It was not a perfect bill, but it has reduced air pollution substantially. A "cap and trade" approach that was opposed by some environmentalists at the time resulted in reduced compliance costs well below anyone's lowest projections and is now a model for climate change emissions control. The legislation was highly cost-effective. Thirteen years later, during the George W. Bush administration, the White House Office of Management and Budget estimated that each dollar invested in clean air had resulted in eight dollars in benefits. Additional pollution reductions put forward by the Obama administration to reduce fine particulate soot emissions are projected to save thirty dollars in health care costs for every dollar invested.

Clearly, we are much better off than we would have been if the 1970 and 1990 Clean Air Acts had not passed. There are three times more cars on the road today, but pollution levels are much lower. The air is cleaner than it was. This legislation is now held out as a great success story. But would the imperfect 1990 compromise be acceptable if it were being considered today?

The failure of the 2009 Copenhagen Summit on climate change

is another case in point. The Copenhagen Summit's inability to establish any binding limits on climate change pollutants was due to the same failed strategy that occurred at the Rio de Janeiro Earth Summit in 1992 and in the Kyoto Protocol in 1997. By insisting on a comprehensive plan rather than a first-steps common-ground strategy, climate change proponents have repeatedly come away with next to nothing. After twenty years of international meetings, there is no binding agreement for any actions worldwide to alleviate one of the greatest threats humanity has ever faced. The world is not ready for a forty-year plan but just may be ready to start taking a cost-effective series of first steps.

Climate change abatement needs to start with a "no regrets plan" whereby the world of nations agrees to binding commitments to take all of the measures that both reduce greenhouse gases and benefit the world economy. There is not a downside to this approach. The business consulting giant McKinsey and Company, as well as others, tell us that the first steps to reduce concentrations of carbon dioxide and other greenhouse gases are highly cost-effective. They show that improving energy efficiency just with existing technologies (where there is an internal rate of return of 10 percent or more) would cut the US energy bill by 23 percent and save a net $680 billion by 2020. Similar savings are estimated for the rest of the world. These measures would contribute substantially to the greenhouse gas emission abatement to limit warming to the Copenhagen accord target of 2 degrees C. This is not a far-fetched goal. Some major companies, such as DuPont, have already achieved this level of cost-effective energy reduction. New and emerging technologies will make much more possible.

Implementing these measures would provide the world with real projects for the next decade that would yield real pollution reduction—at net cost savings. During this time both new scientific knowledge on impacts and new technologies for pollution reductions can inform our next steps. Even the most skeptical of the climate change opponents should be able to agree to an insurance policy of first steps that also provides an economic return—an insurance policy that we are paid to take. What if the world had agreed to a strategy like this in Rio in 1992 or Kyoto in 1997? Would we be well on our way to real reductions of greenhouse gases, with real-world examples of environmental and economic benefits there to drive the next round of cuts, rather than another round of nonbinding and unenforceable goals?

Gridlock on the issue of population control causes much avoidable human suffering and environmental damage. Making modern contraception available to women would also reduce newborn and maternal deaths and reduce by millions the number of abortions every year.

Conservation is full of complex issues that do not benefit from overly simplistic solutions or ideological rhetoric. For example, almost any timber harvest, and even many thinning programs designed to protect homes and lives, face oppositional appeals from some environmentalists. Timber harvest in national forests was too high during the 1980s at over twelve billion board feet and dropped to below two billion board feet by the end of the 1990s. For environmental reasons alone, not to mention jobs and the trade deficit, this is arguably too low. About 75 percent of America's forest products come from nations with lower forestry standards than ours. When we do not harvest sustainably here, we do not eliminate environmental impact. Instead, we export the impacts—and exacerbate them.

The same thing can be said for oil development. Our imported oil inevitably comes from nations with lower environmental standards and worse enforcement than we have in the United States. Nigeria, for instance, has suffered spills equal to the Exxon Valdez every year since 1969 and has two thousand active spills today. When we do not use oil more efficiently, or when shortsighted development practices lead to opposition to domestic drilling, that demand does not disappear. When we import oil we do not eliminate environmental impacts, we export them. When we do not use readily available cost-effective technology to reduce the amount of oil we consume, or refuse to drill responsibly at home, we import oil and export spills to places even less capable of handling them. When the ban on drilling in the Gulf of Mexico was implemented following the Deepwater Horizon disaster in April of 2010, many of the gulf's oilrigs were towed to Africa.

During the 1970s, when much environmental progress was made, leaders in Congress and the national conservation groups took the political support and public opinion available to them and, in most cases, worked together to craft the best compromise solution possible. The nation passed some important, though imperfect, legislation. Critically, in most cases they set a timeframe for reevaluation and "reauthorization" of the new laws as a way to incorporate learning and new information.

In the early 1990s, this dynamic changed. Both sides became hardened. Compromise became synonymous with cowardice. Kindness was mistaken for weakness. Some of the more radical Republican leaders attempted to roll back long-standing proven protections under the so-called "Contract with America." At the same time, national environmental leaders came under intense criticism for any thought of compromise and were accused of being out of touch with their grassroots. If they had any inclination to make the best deal that public opinion and political will made possible, they were accused of being too close to power, too accommodating, and even too professional. Environmental leaders who adopted the proven strategy for success by negotiating responsibly or considering compromise to obtain the best deal possible at the time faced ridicule or worse. Some even lost their jobs due to efforts to work across political parties or constituencies. We tend to celebrate the most passionate and charismatic defenders of the faith, not the most strategic and effective dealmakers who are responsible for the most progress.

A lack of civility in the rhetoric and tactics used by some groups on both sides of the debate also plays a large role in the stalemate on many current environmental issues. Ironically, when applied within the environmental community this same incivility drives dedicated volunteers away from participation with groups and issues. We use science to determine environmental goals and desired outcomes but often use little science as we allow emotion to determine strategies for implementing progress. The best cognitive science on messaging tells us that when communications about the environment are too extreme, too dire, or too partisan, large segments of the public tune out and dismiss the message. Presenting solutions, expressing concern about lost opportunities, or engaging Americans in "can do" thinking are better ways to generate interest in conservation, find solutions, and get them implemented.

It is no coincidence that one of the greatest state victories for conservation in history, a dedicated $7.5 billion for water quality and wildlife, was based on the tradition of human neighborliness called "Minnesota nice." In 2008, after a ten-year grassroots citizen effort to get the measure on the ballot, Minnesota voters passed a 3/8 percent sales tax dedicated to conservation. It yields over $270 million per year for habitat restoration and land conservation. Over twenty-five years of the program, this will total a $7.5 billion investment in Minnesota's natural heritage. When duck hunters and bird watchers stuck together through years of adversity and finally got the compromise initiative on the ballot, it passed by the widest margin of any Minnesota statewide election in history, 57 to 39 percent, with sixty-one thousand more votes than President Obama received. They accomplished this during the depth of the worst recession in seventy-five years.

The stunning success of the nation's land trusts' efforts at open space and habitat conservation is another great example of the power of a positive approach. Land trusts are land conservation organizations that usually work in local communities. In 1980, there were only a few land trusts in existence. Today, there are about 1,700 land trusts. Over thirty-seven million acres—an area equal to sixteen Yellowstone Parks—have been privately and voluntarily protected in just over thirty years. Over the past twenty years, during a time when opposition to taxes has become a gospel for some, voters have approved fifty-six billion dollars in local tax increases for open-space bonds and other land conservation initiatives. When given the chance, Americans will vote for conservation solutions—even if it means a self-imposed tax increase.

Polling shows that land conservation initiatives are popular everywhere, even in states where local politics prevent citizens from having the right to vote on them. In Idaho, for example, a state with particularly strong anti-tax sentiments, polls show strong support and willingness to pay twenty dollars per year per person for dedicated funds for land conservation. When presented thoughtfully, conservation has overwhelming and widespread appeal.

If you look at the campaign materials for these land conservation initiatives, you see little strident rhetoric and a lot of practical solutions. When we move the conservation debate away from polemics to practical solutions, we usually succeed. We need a strategic approach to environmental protection that embraces this principle and does a better job of finding and implementing solutions. The success of land conservation provides a striking contrast to the gridlock of the last twenty years on environmental issues and the recent declines in environmentalists' popularity.

Constructive engagement with business may be the most critical factor to conservation success overall. Paul Hawken, author of *The Ecology of Commerce* said it best: "Ironically, business contains our blessing. It must, because no other institution in the modern world is powerful enough to foster the necessary changes." Even more to the point, Jared Diamond, the Pulitzer Prize–winning author, said in *Collapse: How Societies Choose to Fail or Succeed*: "My view is that, if environmentalists aren't willing to engage with big businesses, which are the most powerful forces in the modern world, it won't be possible to solve the world's environmental problems." There is no doubt that some business practices have been shortsighted, stupid, or even criminal, but business is not a monolith. We need to find and support enlightened leaders. We cannot succeed without them.

Done right, environmental excellence is good business and good for business. Conservation is essentially a best business practice. It seeks to maximize return on the investment of a natural asset, while minimizing the depreciation of natural capital. It pushes companies to take a more long-range view—past the typical time horizon of a quarterly or annual report. When we use our natural resource assets faster than we renew them, or ignore the very real costs of pollution downriver or downwind, we record illusory gains in income and mask permanent losses in wealth. Environmentally conscious business practices can also help us to stabilize the economy. For example, every economic downturn since 1973 has been preceded by sharp increases in the price of oil. Price spikes alone are estimated to have cost the economy seven trillion dollars. Energy efficiency and conservation are as good for the economy and national security as they are for the environment.

Almost every major step forward in conservation was a bipartisan compromise that was crafted from the middle. So why is compromise now synonymous with cowardice? Partisan rivals with harsh campaigns can usually stop each other's initiatives, but durable progress requires a strong majority. We cannot succeed without each other. The prospects for success on any issue are directly proportional to the broadness of the base of support. Practically speaking, and functionally in the case of the US Senate, a supermajority is needed to make durable progress on any issue. Yet in a mission-driven field like conservation, what leader wants to be known as the great compromiser? It is those who are willing to step out from the comfort of their clique and engage with others who are almost always most responsible for making progress.

In the face of this persistent reality of environmental success and failure, environmentalists must own their inconvenient truth—radical environmentalism is effectively anti-environmental. All of our experiences in environmental policymaking show that while an ideological approach can help identify a problem, or maybe even stop a bad idea, it cannot succeed in building the support needed for positive progress. Even worse, a strident or demonizing approach on one issue alienates natural allies on other issues where there is common ground and where support is needed. Ironically, the same rhetoric that grabs media attention and excites environmental believers works against harnessing the diversity of support needed to accomplish something positive.

If a century of conservation practice shows that a divisive ideological approach rather than an inclusive strategic approach to conservation will assure failure, can proponents of this approach really claim to be environmental leaders? Is there another motivation at work? Is a moral or highly principled position either moral or principled if it is being promoted by a demonstrably failed strategy that will not result in more long-term and durable improvement in environmental conservation?

The case for environmental protection is itself a great one, full of compelling examples of smart solutions that benefit people, the environment, and the economy at the same time. Americans, and people all over the world, want environmentally positive solutions. The United Nations Environment Program points out that "In 2008–9, the world's governments rapidly mobilized hundreds of billions of dollars to prevent collapse of a financial system whose flimsy foundations took the markets by surprise. Now we have clear warnings of the potential breaking points towards which we are pushing the ecosystems that have shaped our civilizations. For a fraction of the money summoned up instantly to avoid economic meltdown, we can avoid a much more serious and fundamental breakdown in the Earth's life support systems."

Polarization and incivility are rapidly destroying the fabric of our nation and its environment. We need to stop using our issues, as right as they may be, as cudgels with which to bludgeon those who have not come to the exact same conclusions as we have. If we want to save the planet and assure future generations of a quality of life, we must be willing to engage with each other and compromise. This is what has worked in the past and what will work in the future. If we are serious about conservation, we must be equally serious about strategic compromise. Many people care about the environment, but some of the most active are pursuing dead-end strategies that will only assure continued failure. Environmentalists are great at describing problems, not as good at explaining solutions, and oftentimes so passionate about their cause that they are terrible at thinking and acting strategically. In the pages that follow are many powerful examples of extraordinary success using a strategy of civil engagement and compromise.

3
The Conservation of Hope

The Ozone Hole, Acid Rain, and Climate Change

It is not too late. God's world has incredible healing powers.
Within a single generation, we could steer the earth
toward our children's future. Let that generation start now.
—Pope John Paul II and Patriarch Bartholomew I,
2002 Proclamation in Optimism and Prayer

Nothing in the world can take the place of persistence. Talent will not;
nothing is more common than unsuccessful men with talent. Genius will not;
unrewarded genius is almost a proverb. Education will not; the world is
full of educated derelicts. Persistence alone is omnipotent.
—Calvin Coolidge

IN BOTH CASES, it took ten years to do it. During the 1980s, people came together with persistence and determination and built major solutions to two of the most vexing environmental issues the world has ever known: control of chemicals that deplete stratospheric ozone and control of the pollutants that cause acid rain. These issues were resolved by bipartisan compromise during two Republican presidencies. The positive resolution of these two complex and difficult issues gives us hope and a model of success for the future on climate change and other issues.

THE OZONE HOLE

It never makes the news broadcasts or headlines, but we already saved the earth once. We did it based on a cooperative framework that relied on science. Back in the 1980s, broad-based support for a bipartisan effort succeeded in developing a timeline for the elimination of chemicals that deplete the atmospheric ozone layer that protects the Earth from harmful ultraviolet radiation.

In 1974, two chemists named Sherwood Rowland and Mario Molina published a scientific paper showing how a popular class of industrial chemicals called chlorofluorocarbons (CFCs) was depleting the ozone layer in the Earth's stratosphere. Their work won them the Nobel Prize. It also saved the Earth.

The ozone layer filters out harmful ultraviolet rays from the sun—making life on Earth possible. Though generally unknown to the public at the time, CFC compounds were used widely in refrigerators and air conditioners, foam packaging, as propellants in aerosols, and elsewhere. CFCs were developed in the 1930s as an alternative to dangerous substances like ammonia and sulfur dioxide, which were commonly used as refrigerants at the time. Non-toxic, non-flammable, and non-reactive with other chemical compounds, CFCs were ideal in many applications. Their use grew steadily for half a century.

As the scientific community gathered evidence of ozone depletion and the seriousness of the threat became apparent, public pressure mounted for greater controls on CFCs. Industrial leaders initially balked at the notion of ending CFC production. It was a common refrain. No acceptable alternatives were on the shelf, they said, and finding substitutes would be costly, slow, and could reduce performance. At worst, they feared a ban could disrupt the US economy severely. CFCs were deeply embedded in US industry. By 1987, goods and services involving CFCs were worth more than $28 billion annually. More than $128 billion of installed equipment relied on these chemicals.

As with climate change today, most of the world's serious business and political leaders became convinced that CFCs posed a severe threat to life on Earth. In 1978, the US government took early action with a ban on "non-essential" aerosol products containing CFCs. By

1987, world leaders agreed on a dramatic course of comprehensive action. In the Montreal Protocol of Substances that Deplete the Ozone Layer, it was agreed that chemical manufacturers would phase out the production of CFCs for use in the developed nations. There is a slightly more relaxed timetable for developing nations.

As it turned out, the CFC phase-out has not been insurmountable. With considerable human ingenuity, enough lead time, and capital investment, many US industries eliminated the use of CFCs more quickly, at lower cost, and with more related environmental benefits than anyone thought possible. Today, production and use of CFCs has been reduced by over 95 percent since 1988. The presence of these chlorine compounds in the stratosphere is decreasing. The ozone hole is getting smaller. CFCs will be effectively eliminated from the atmosphere by 2100.

As we see today on climate change, no amount of independent scientific data could convince everyone that the threat posed by CFCs was real and the solutions viable. The Montreal Protocol was accomplished despite a last-minute attempt to sabotage the agreement by two leading members of Congress named, ironically, DeLay and Doolittle. In late 1986, Rep. Tom DeLay, a Republican from Texas, and Rep. John Doolittle, a Republican from California, introduced legislation to repeal the CFC ban altogether. DeLay was House majority whip, the third-highest-ranking member. He had first made headlines by declaring that the pesticide DDT was not harmful. Years later, in November of 2010, he was convicted on violations of campaign finance law and money laundering. DeLay and Doolittle dismissed as insufficient the large body of evidence linking CFCs to ozone depletion. In response, a representative from DuPont, at that time the world's largest manufacturer of CFCs replied, "We at DuPont know as much about the scientific aspects of these chemicals as anybody in the world. We have concluded that turning back the phase-out at this point would be totally counterproductive."

ACID RAIN

Martin Pfeiffer called them "biostitutes," biologists who prostituted their science for big utilities who denied that their coal-fired power plants were killing his Adirondack lakes. Pfeiffer was a regional fisheries biologist in New York State and one of the first North American scientists to document the degradation of aquatic habitat throughout much of the eastern United States and Canada. Scottish chemist Robert Angus Smith first discovered and named acid rain in 1852. By the early 1980s, Harold Harvey and other Canadian scientists confirmed what Pfeiffer and scientists in Scandinavia already knew. Acid rain was killing their lakes as well. Subsequent research found that the sources of the pollution could be many hundreds of miles away and that the damage was not just limited to lakes. Forests, buildings, amphibians, waterfowl, and even human health were being negatively affected.

It took ten years of bipartisan effort in both the United States and Canada, but by 1990 both nations passed new laws to significantly curtail the emissions that cause acid rain. In the United States, it is the last time major pollution control legislation passed and became law. Many people worked very hard on this issue, but it would not have happened without strong bipartisan support in the United States and Canada. In the United States there was leadership from both parties. In the House, Reps. Henry Waxman (D-CA) and Gerry Sikorski (D-MN) led the way. In the Senate, much of the leadership came from Republicans: Robert Stafford (R-VT), David Durenberger (R-MN) and John Chaffee (R-RI). Pres. Ronald Reagan showed little interest in the issue, despite years of pleas from Canada and his fellow conservative and Irishman, Prime Minister Brian Mulroney. A political cartoon in Canada showed the prime minister imploring the president to do something: "Mr. President, the people of Canada pray for an end to acid rain." "Well Brian, tell them that Nancy and I join them in their prayers." The breakthrough came when Pres. George H. W. Bush and his Environmental Protection Agency administrator, noted conservationist William K. Reilly, brokered a compromise that led to passage of the 1990 Clean Air Act and its acid rain title. It would not have happened without years of work and the support of two of Canada's conservative members of Parliament.

In Canada, the most persistent leadership came from an obscure backbench member of Parliament (MP) best known for his unsuccessful support of restoring capital punishment in Canada, the Hon. Stan Darling. Past normal retirement age, Stan Darling represented the district of Muskoka-Haliburton, an area of pristine lakes nestled in granitic bedrock that provided little buffering for the onslaught of pollution from both Canada and the United States. As in the Adirondack Mountains of northern New York State, it was one of the first places to understand the impact of acid rain. Like Martin Pfeiffer in New York, Stan Darling was never shy about speaking out—no matter who it was or which party they came from. In Washington, DC, Ottawa, or wherever he was, Stan Darling became North America's most determined advocate for acid rain control. Polite and persistent, he became chair of his nation's special parliamentary committee on acid rain. Stan even coaxed an agreement out of Ronald Reagan to do something about acid rain—the only person to do so—even though President Reagan never made good on his promise. Late in 1990, when Pres. George H. W. Bush and Prime Minister Brian Mulroney signed a US-Canada treaty on acid rain on Parliament Hill in Ottawa, Stan Darling was the overwhelming choice to be given the pen used by the two heads of state to sign the accord.

A former soldier and avid outdoorsman, John Fraser was a member of Parliament from British Columbia. He is an expert on Canada's military and on the environment. In 1980, with Stan Darling and others, he helped start a citizen group called the Canadian Coalition on Acid Rain, who hired two young and talented activists—Adele Hurley and Michael Perley. At the time, Fraser was Canada's environment critic—the MP from the minority party that monitored and critiqued the environment minister. On the acid rain issue, however, Canada spoke with one voice, and Fraser would often speak to important audiences in the United States and Canada on behalf of the environment minister. John Fraser was known and respected as an honest, thoughtful, and fair-minded legislator. Soon after the Conservatives were voted into the majority in 1986 under Prime Minister Brian Mulroney, Fraser became Canada's first freely elected Speaker of the House. As the arbitrator of the House of Commons, the Speaker "was not allowed to have an original thought in his head," as Fraser liked to joke. But he set the agenda for the House of Commons and decided who would speak and who would not. Those who needed to speak on acid rain were always heard, and those of us who were working on the issue had a friend who was the fourth-highest-ranking person in Canada's government paying close attention. Canada led the way on acid rain control in North America and convinced the United States to act.

On November 15, 1990, the 1990 US Clean Air Act revision became law. Included in Title IV was a requirement that the sulfur and nitrogen dioxide emissions that cause acid rain would be reduced by ten million tons—a 40 percent reduction. The final legislative language on acid rain included a "cap and trade" approach that was proposed by the Environmental Defense Fund but opposed by many other environmentalists at the time. This mechanism allowed polluters to trade emissions credits in a way that allowed industry to prioritize which plants to cut emissions first in order to achieve the lowest total cost. Emissions trading resulted in reduced compliance costs well below the lowest projections. It was extremely effective and has become the model for greenhouse gas reduction "cap and trade" mechanism. During the debates leading up to passage of the 1990 Clean Air Act, the utilities responsible for most of the pollution estimated it would cost $1,500 per ton to reduce the pollution that caused acid rain. EPA estimated that the cost would be between $600 and $800 per ton. Environmentalists estimated the costs to be only $300 per ton. We were all wrong. Over the next decade, the actual cost of removing ten million tons of sulfur dioxide per year from the air was less than $200 per ton.

Thirteen years after the Clean Air Act of 1990, in 2003, the George W. Bush administration's White House Office of Management and Budget (OMB) estimated that each dollar invested in clean air had resulted in eight dollars in benefits. The report, *The Costs and Benefits of Regulation,* was the most comprehensive federal study ever on regulatory costs and benefits. The official responsible was Dr. John B. Graham, a former Harvard professor and an authority on cost-benefit analysis. Many Washington, DC, environmental groups, some of whom had opposed his confirmation to his post at OMB, did not consider Graham a friend of the environment. Upon release of the report, Graham said, "Our role at OMB is to report the best available estimates of benefits and costs, regardless of whether this information favors one advocacy group or another. In this case, the data show that EPA's clean-air office has issued some highly beneficial rules."

In fact, the report provided data on 107 major federal rules dealing with agriculture, education, energy, health and human services, housing, labor, transportation, and the environment. In all cases, the benefits of regulation exceeded the costs. EPA regulations provided the largest payback, with clean air regulations on top of all. The analysis conducted by a Republican "green eyeshade" economist from Harvard found that major federal regulations provide benefits of from $135 billion to $218 billion annually, while costing taxpayers between $38 billion and $44 billion. Federal regulations enforcing the EPA's clean air and water laws accounted for the majority of the regulatory benefits to the public estimated over the last decade. Clean water regulations accounted for benefits of up to $8 billion at a cost of $2.4 to $2.9 billion. Clean air regulations provided up to $163 billion in benefits, while costing society only about $21 billion. This is almost an eightfold return on investment.

This strong economic outcome shows the folly of kneejerk anti-regulatory behavior. Some regulations are highly cost-effective. Emissions trading was developed by Republicans in the 1980s and opposed by many liberals. Today, emissions trading is supported by liberals and called "cap and tax" by Republicans. Both sides should support innovative methods to reduce the costs of regulations to make them more efficient.

In early 2005, EPA reported on the environmental success of the 1990 Clean Air Act. By the end of 2004, sulfur dioxide concentrations plummeted throughout the eastern United States. Emissions of sulfur dioxide dropped by 35 percent and nitrogen oxide by 45 percent. This was accomplished at the same time that net electrical generation rose by 25 percent, and the average net cost of electricity dropped by over 10 percent.

By late 2005, the George W. Bush administration issued the Clean Air Interstate Rule to reduce emissions by another 70 percent from 2003 levels—again using emissions trading to lower compliance costs. It was estimated that the benefits of this round of pollution reduction would exceed cost of compliance by twenty-five times. Predictably, this sensible approach was unacceptable to hardheads on both sides. It was not strong enough for some environmentalists and too strong for some industry. Unfortunately, legislation to codify this approach was not supported by some environmentalists so the legislation never passed in Congress. When the Bush administration tried to tighten air pollution standards under existing law, several utilities led by the Southern Company sued them. The courts invalidated the clean air rule as going beyond EPA authority. This decision went beyond what the utilities had hoped for, leaving them with an uncertain regulatory future and Americans with dirtier air. When Bush left office, the Clean Air Interstate rule was still being reformulated.

Today, we have a chance to take the lessons learned from the acid rain campaign and the Montreal Protocol and use them to begin to address the environmental plague of our time—climate change.

CLIMATE CHANGE

First of all, the problem of climate change goes well beyond "global warming." That is but one symptom of a much more complex problem and a symptom that is embedded in very complex patterns of natural temperature fluctuations. Even though warming is driving much of the change, weather intensity and changes in weather patterns and climate will have just as profound an impact. This issue presents a great challenge, perhaps the greatest ever faced by Earth's inhabitants. It can be greatly alleviated by human ingenuity and better utilization of today's technology, not to mention tomorrow's. Who would have imagined the advances of just the last twenty years in computer technology alone? There is plenty of reason to hope for a solution to climate change, but yesterday's tactics are not getting us there.

The world has held three major international summits, and a number of smaller ones, to try to come up with a plan to address climate change. The Copenhagen Summit in 2009 started with great expectations and ended with no agreement to establish any binding limits on climate change pollutants. This is due to the same failed strategy that occurred at the Rio de Janeiro Earth Summit in 1992 and during the Kyoto Protocol in 1997. By insisting on a comprehensive plan rather than a first-steps strategy, climate change proponents have come away with next to nothing. While an ambitious goal is appropriate, the world is not ready for a forty-year plan or even a twenty-year plan but might be ready for a cost-effective five- or ten-year plan to get started. Given the rapid pace of technological change alone, planning horizons in many endeavors are being reduced. The world of nations urgently needs to begin to address this problem by taking advantage of the many cost-effective opportunities we have available to us, even if we cannot agree on a complete plan. The International Energy Agency, in *World Energy Outlook, 2012* reports that if world governments just adopted cost-effective, off-the-shelf techniques to cut energy use, energy-related carbon dioxide emissions would peak in

2020 and would decline from there. We can learn from our success and continue to move forward informed by new technologies and science.

Art Rosenfeld is one of the world's top experts on energy efficiency and its ability to cost-effectively abate climate change. He is a founder of the Lawrence Berkeley National Lab and on the board of the California Energy Commission. In the *Wall Street Journal* on Earth Day 2010, Art pointed out that simply painting every eligible flat roof white would, over the life of the buildings, save enough energy to reduce emissions equal to not using 40 percent of the world's cars for fifteen years or turning off the entire world's emissions for four months. Still, after twenty years and many international conferences we still do not have a global agreement to take simple steps like this.

According to the business consulting giant McKinsey and Company, taking the first steps to address climate change by improving energy efficiency with existing technology would cut the US energy bill by 23 percent and save a net $680 billion by 2020. This could be done using only today's off-the-shelf technology whose use yields a 10 percent return on investment. For years, McKinsey and Company, as well as others, have demonstrated that these first steps to reduce concentrations of carbon dioxide and other greenhouse gases are highly cost-effective. Efficiencies in building insulation, commercial vehicles, air conditioning, and lighting provide the greatest savings. These are not estimates from the Sierra Club or the Democratic Party; these come from one of the nation's blue-chip corporate management firms.

Implementing these measures would provide the world with real projects for the next decade that would yield real pollution reductions. During this time both new science on impacts and new technologies for reductions can inform our next steps. Even the most skeptical of the climate change opponents should be able to agree to a no-cost insurance policy of first steps. If the world had agreed to a strategy like this in Rio in 1992 or Kyoto in 1997, would we be well on our way to real reductions, rather than another round of unenforceable goals?

There is an abundance of cost-effective opportunities for reducing greenhouse gases. Today's hybrid vehicles get about 30 percent better mileage than the same car that is not a hybrid but account for only about 3 percent of the vehicle fleet on the road. Over the life of the vehicle, my hybrid sport utility vehicle will return two to three times the additional cost of the hybrid engine in fuel savings. I save about eight hundred dollars per year in gas over a standard model. The extra four thousand dollars I paid was paid back in five years. I kept my last car for fifteen years, which would mean an eight thousand dollar net return on the extra cost incurred by this hybrid SUV. That is about a nine percent per year return—three times what my retirement fund has averaged over the last twelve years—for driving a car that pollutes less, reduces dependence on foreign oil, and reduces the foreign trade deficit. Today, hybrids are available in a variety of sizes for all the basic automobile models: sedans, sport utility vehicles, and pick-up trucks. Even the federal vehicle fleet, where cost savings would be quick and obvious, only uses hybrids for 2 percent of its fleet.

Clean diesel engines, a popular option in Europe, can do almost as well. An Ethanol Boosting System developed at the Massachusetts Institute of Technology that injects small amounts of supplemental ethanol into the combustion chamber could provide similar efficiencies at even less cost. The new generation of plug-in hybrids will be an order of magnitude even more efficient than hybrids or advanced diesel, as will electronic vehicles, but so far market penetration is tiny.

In August of 2012, Pres. Barack Obama and thirteen automakers announced an agreement to substantially increase the efficiency of America's automobile fleet. They agreed to raise the Corporate Average Fuel Economy (CAFE) to 54.5 miles per gallon by 2025. After setting a standard in 1975 of 27.5 miles per gallon by 1985 (it was reached in 1990), the standard had remained unimproved despite significant advances in technology. By 2025, the new CAFE standards are estimated to have saved the United States $1.8 trillion. This will reduce oil consumption by 2.1 million barrels per day, which is equivalent to half of the OPEC import in 2012. By 2025, this will cut sixty-one billion tons of greenhouse gas emissions, equal to the total emitted by the United States in 2010.

Although smaller devices and appliances, notably televisions and personal computers, offer only 19 percent of the 2020 residential opportunity for energy savings, capturing that savings would require just $3.4 billion in incremental capital with possible savings of $65 billion, according to the McKinsey analysts. For appliances, mandatory standards saved US consumers $30 billion in energy bills from 1987 to 2005, even though standards were implemented for only a few of the appliances that were required. Computers, medical and lab equipment, cash registers, and data servers offer more cost-effective opportunities: savings of $57 billion for an $8 billion investment.

Former CIA director Jim Woolsey does a great job outlining the national security benefits of energy efficiency and locally produced energy. He makes a strong case that both tree-huggers and national defense hawks should rally behind efforts to use energy more wisely. Every economic downturn since 1973 has been preceded by sharp increases in the price of oil, costing the economy $7 trillion. Efficiency and locally produced energy are not likely to be vulnerable to wild price swings, international instability, or acts of terrorism. He points out that "combined heat and power," the beneficial use of waste heat from power plants or industry, provides almost 50 percent of Denmark's electricity needs but only 8 percent in the United States. It is not technology but culture and outdated regulations that prevent us from using energy that we currently waste. Woolsey also believes that climate change is likely "to dominate" US security and humanitarian concerns while making it more difficult to supply the kind of generous and professional assistance we have provided to disasters over the years. He points out that energy efficiency also helps the war on terror, "the only war we have ever fought in which we are funding both sides."

Emerging technologies are even more exciting. The world's most secure "new" energy source may also be our most mundane and our greenest—our garbage. This energy rich feedstock costs nothing to produce. It does not need to be mined, drilled, cultivated, or even collected from the sun or wind. It is most abundant where energy is most needed. People pay you to take it.

During the 1970s and 80s, waste-to-energy projects were held out as a panacea. They depended on loosely controlled incineration, which was often incomplete. Most of the plants were a disaster. They burned and volatilized heavy metals and other toxins, spreading them across the landscape. Today, there is a promising array of new technologies that do much better. This is an energy source we should not ignore.

In 2007, the United States produced 254 million tons of municipal solid waste. After recycling and composting, 137 million tons of energy-rich waste was discarded to landfills or other disposal. Depending on the effectiveness of glass and metal recycling, municipal solid waste has an energy value between 5500 and 8000 BTUs per pound. For comparison, coal has an energy value of about 9000 BTUs per pound and lignite about 7000 BTUs per pound. Instead of using this energy-rich waste to pollute our land, water, and air, it should be used to create energy and jobs here in the United States. There is a new generation of transformative technologies that allows waste to be safely and cleanly converted into clean fuel energy.

For example, InEnTec LLC's Plasma Enhanced Melter™ (PEM™) is a technology based on research by Massachusetts Institute of Technology and Battelle Pacific Northwest National Laboratory scientists. Using a unique combination of proven technologies, this process converts garbage to energy-rich gas and safe recyclable byproducts. This eliminates air and groundwater pollution due to incineration or landfills. When used to process municipal waste and other energy-rich waste, this technology produces a synthesis gas that is readily catalyzed into liquid fuels such as ethanol. Converting the 137 million tons of post recycled waste—where glass, metal, and high-value plastics are removed—would generate about sixteen billion gallons of ethanol fuel or about 11 percent of the gasoline used each year in the United States.

Converting municipal garbage into fuel can significantly reduce greenhouse gas emissions. The PEM™ generates about 120 gallons of ethanol per ton of garbage and eliminates around 100 pounds of land-fill methane. This is around one ton CO_2 equivalent of greenhouse gas. Methane is a potent greenhouse gas, twenty times more potent than carbon dioxide, and its reduction should have a high priority. EPA identifies methane reductions as having the greatest near-term potential for cost-effective greenhouse gas reductions.

Compared to business as usual, creating usable energy by converting municipal waste to fuel provides not just a carbon neutral energy source. It provides a carbon negative energy source—one that produces energy while reducing greenhouse gases. A prototype in Richland, Washington, was tested using that city's waste, and a commercial pilot project came online in Arlington, Oregon, in late 2012. Since there is much more of it, conversion of industrial waste has an even higher potential than municipal waste. Dow Corning uses one of these facilities to process industrial waste in Midland, Michigan. Hazardous waste is chemically separated and reused on site. This saves energy and chemicals and eliminates over-the-road transportation of hazardous material. Another PEM™ plant has operated for several years in Taiwan to convert medical waste into electrical energy.

In Edmonton, Alberta, a company called Enerkem is building a municipal solid waste-to-biofuels production facility to be completed by 2013. The plant will produce ten million gallons of ethanol per year. Waste Management, the world's largest waste processor, has joint ventures with both Enerkem and InEnTec.

In Europe, four hundred plants are being built to convert trash into energy. These plants are modern incinerators that are almost emission free. Arrays of filters catch pollutants, from mercury to dioxin that would not have been captured only a decade ago. Unfortunately, only a couple of these advanced plants are being built in the United States.

America uses 140 billion gallons of gasoline and 40 billion gallons of diesel fuel per year. We import 36 billion gallons of oil from the Middle East alone. In recent years, our nation's net trade deficit for foreign oil has averaged about $300 billion per year. Investing in systems that convert energy-rich garbage into usable fuel can keep many of those dollars at home, bolstering our economy and providing jobs for hundreds of thousands of Americans.

Using waste as a new source of domestic fuel can also help stabilize the economy. Fuel generated from waste is not likely to be vulnerable to wild price swings, international instability, or acts of terrorism. The International Energy Agency projects that the Organization of Petroleum Exporting Countries (OPEC) revenue will be four times as high in the next twenty years as in the last twenty years.

The best of the new waste-to-energy technologies are built on a modular scale—allowing them to use local waste to make and use fuel locally. This eliminates the need for long-distance trucking of solid waste and fuel, which further reduces greenhouse gases and local air pollutants. If used to generate electricity, it can reduce the need for new power lines. It also makes our highways less congested and safer. Treating waste in this way also reduces a vector for possible disease transmission from animal waste, food waste, offal, carcasses, and other biological contaminants.

Rather than converting land to energy crops or using agricultural commodities for fuel, using waste for energy helps conserve water, reduce water pollution, protect wildlife habitat, and preserve biodiversity. Even more importantly, it takes pressure off world grain prices and the potential starvation of the world's poorest people and the resulting threat to fragile democracies worldwide.

Energy-rich garbage is available in every region. It is most abundant in population centers where fuel demand is highest. As we look for ways to provide clean energy and stimulate the economy, energy-rich waste provides a remarkable opportunity that should not be overlooked.

When you put together new sources of energy like this, and the untapped potential to improve end-use efficiency, you begin to realize that we can take steps to address climate change that will also help the economy. Solar and wind energy can play an important role in some areas. New low-till agricultural methods and other methods of sequestering carbon can also make substantial contributions to reducing carbon in the atmosphere. Most important, however, may be the new technologies that we do not yet know about that will be developed as we put these currently available technologies to use.

Climate change can be abated but only if we take today's technology off the shelf and put it into widespread use. Only 3 percent of the cars on the road use hybrid technology. If we converted the entire fleet, we could alone reduce the nation's fuel use by about 25 percent—more than we import from the entire Persian Gulf. Immediate progress can be made by collective action with the logical and cost-effective first steps: painting some roofs white, making high-return investments in energy efficiency, and using our garbage to make fuel rather than letting it sit in landfills generating climate change gases.

4

Population

The Fundamental Issue

The Earth's population could double in the next 40 years,
creating immense hunger, unemployment, civil unrest
and environmental destruction.
—Charlton Heston, actor, spokesman for
the National Rifle Association

Growth for its own sake is the ideology of the cancer cell.
—Edward Abbey, author and environmentalist

A MAN HAD A HOME BY THE RIVER, and one day a flood came. As the water reached his porch, a rescue boat came by. "Get in," the boatman yelled. "No," said the homeowner, "I believe that God will protect me." Hours later, the water was up to the second floor and the boat came back. The homeowner again refused a ride. "I have faith in the Lord," he said. Finally, standing on his chimney, he faithfully waved off an attempt by a helicopter to save him. Then he drowned. When he came before God in heaven the homeowner asked, "How could this happen? I believed in you and you let me die." God replied, "I don't know what you are talking about; I sent out two boats and a helicopter."

When I was born in 1952, there were fewer than three billion people on Earth. Today there are seven billion. If I live seventy-eight years—the average life expectancy for white males—then in the year 2030 when I depart the planet there likely will be more than nine billion of us, and maybe as many as ten to twelve billion.

Current rates of population growth cause great suffering, pose significant risks to human well-being, and have an overwhelming impact on the natural world. More than a quarter of the world's people live in extreme poverty now, and half of those are starving. Even with great advances in technology and increases in agricultural production, the Earth cannot handle the load. The world's human carrying capacity is the fundamental issue facing humanity and nature today.

Millions of people want to limit the size of their families. Helping them to do so is probably our only chance of preventing catastrophe for all of us. Thankfully, at the precise moment in human history where we are about to overwhelm our planet with our numbers, we have the means to do something about it. We have our "two boats and a helicopter" but have refused to use them to save ourselves. Safe, cheap and effective contraceptive technology appeared on the planet at the very instant in human history when it was needed. Why is this not viewed as a divinely given and timely gift? Why is something that can prevent so much suffering being held hostage by polarized views of the abortion debate?

The abortion issue is one of the most emotionally charged and intractable issues on Earth. There is not going to be agreement on the abortion issue anytime soon, but an agreement on contraception should be possible. Both sides of the abortion debate would benefit from voluntary widespread access to contraception, which can be made available for very little cost. By investing as little as an additional $3.6 billion per year, the world could provide modern contraception to the more than 215 million women who desire it but cannot obtain it. This would avert annually 640,000 newborn deaths and 150,000 maternal deaths, and would prevent 600,000 children from losing their mothers. It would prevent 25 million abortions every year. In nations where contraception has become available, abortion rates have plummeted.

The 1984 Mexico City policy prohibits foreign organizations that receive US family planning assistance money from using their own funds to counsel or refer for abortion, provide legal abortion, or to work for the legalization of abortion in their country. The policy is an Executive Order first announced by Pres. Ronald Reagan. It was rescinded by Pres. Bill Clinton in 1993, and then it was reinstated by Pres. George Bush on his first day in office in 2001. Pres. Barack Obama rescinded the order on his third day in office in 2009. That is a lot of repealing the repeal of the repeal for an order that is already covered by existing federal law. Since 1973, the Helms amendment to the Foreign Assistance Act has prohibited the use of US funds for abortion services. Using US funds for biomedical research on abortion and lobbying on abortion has been prohibited since 1981. In thirty-five years, no violations have been reported. Nonetheless, this issue has done more than anything else to prevent the provision of contraception to people who need it.

If right wing icon Charlton Heston and left wing writer Ed Abbey can agree on the fundamentals of the need to reduce human population, maybe there is hope that both sides of the abortion debate can find the common ground needed that would prevent extensive human suffering and save lives. Both groups could alleviate a great deal of pain by engaging and working out a compromise to get past the abortion funding issue so they can work together to fund the family planning assistance needed. At stake are 22 million fewer unwanted pregnancies, 25 million fewer abortions, and 150,000 maternal deaths per year. This would also reduce the incidence of HIV AIDS, hunger, ecosystem destruction, and wildlife degradation in some of the most desperate regions of the world.

5

Green and God

The Environment of Faith

God said: "This is the sign of the covenant that I make
between me and you and every living creature
that is with you, for all generations."
—Gen. 9:12

IT IS SAID that during the cultural revolution of the 1960s and 1970s the right took God and the left took green. Fortunately, if that was ever true, it is changing. Today, many faiths have come together to support protection of the natural world, and some of the strongest advocates are also some of the most devoted.

The support is also widespread. The Coalition on the Environment and Jewish Life, the US Conference of Catholic Bishops, the National Council of Churches of Christ, and the Evangelical Environmental Network came together to form the National Religious Partnership on the Environment. They proclaim that "Love and gratitude for God's creation lie deep within religious life. From mountaintops to forests, green pastures to still waters, stars in the sky and lilies of the field, we experience the grace of our Creator and the gift of our presence here.

With Earth in grave environmental peril, many religious Americans are seeking to respond through our faith."

Internationally, some of the highest religious leaders in the world have spoken clearly and unequivocally. His All Holiness, Bartholomew, archbishop of Constantinople, New Rome and Ecumenical Patriarch is the 270th successor to the Apostle Andrew and spiritual leader of 300 million Orthodox Christians worldwide. He says that degradation of the environment, extinction, and pollution are "sins" and that "the environment is not only a political issue; it is also—indeed, it is primarily—a spiritual issue." The late Pope John Paul II said, "The ecological crisis is a moral issue." In 2002, the two spiritual leaders signed an unprecedented declaration that "proclaimed in optimism and prayer" their conclusion that:

> It is not too late. God's world has incredible healing powers. Within a single generation, we could steer the earth toward our children's future. Let that generation start now.
>
> Because now is the *kairos*—the decisive moment in human history, when we can truly make a difference.
>
> Because now is the *kairos*—when the consciousness of the world is rising to the challenge.
>
> Because now is the *kairos*—for us to save the soul of our planet.
>
> Because now is the *kairos*—there is no other day than this day, this time, this moment.
>
> Indeed, let it start now.
>
> May God bless all of us to bring our labors to fruition.
>
> Thank you.

The sense of urgency and possibility so clearly stated by these and other leading religious leaders provide a stark contrast to the war of words that often characterizes environmental debate. There is hope and an eagerness to start now by taking real steps that begin to "steer the earth toward our children's future."

The Evangelical Environmental Network (EEN) is a nonprofit organization in the United States "that seeks to educate, inspire, and mobilize Christians in their effort to care for God's creation, to be faithful stewards of God's provision, and to advocate for actions and policies that honor God and protect the environment. EEN's work is grounded in the Bible's teaching on the responsibility of God's people to 'tend the garden' and in a desire to be faithful to Jesus Christ and to follow Him. EEN publishes materials to equip and inspire individuals, families, and churches; and seeks to educate and mobilize people to make a difference in their churches and communities, and to speak out on national and international policies that affect our ability to preach the Gospel, protect life, and care for God's Creation."

EEN refers to degradations of creation that can be summed up as: "1) land degradation; 2) deforestation; 3) species extinction; 4) water degradation; 5) global toxification; 6) the alteration of atmosphere; 7) human and cultural degradation." They call these degradations signs that "We are pressing against the finite limits God has set for creation. With continued population growth, these degradations will become more severe. Our responsibility is not only to bear and nurture children, but to nurture their home on earth."

Much of the focus of the faith community's interest is properly on the disproportional impact that environmental degradation has on the poor and disadvantaged. Evangelical Christian Jonathan Merritt, the twenty-something author of the book *Green like God: Unlocking the Divine Plan for Our Planet* says, "We are asked by God to act to preserve the planet and to protect the people who depend on the planet's resources."

This awareness is found in Islam as well. "Corruption" it says in the Koran, "has appeared on the land and in the sea because of what the hands of humans have wrought. This is in order that we give them a taste of the consequences of their misdeeds that perhaps they will return to the path of right guidance." Scholars have interpreted "corruption" to mean pollution. "We are Allah's stewards and agents on Earth. We are not masters of this Earth; it does not belong to us to do what we wish. It belongs to Allah and He has entrusted us with its safekeeping."

The foundation of the Jewish relationship with the environment stems from Genesis 2:15: "The Lord God took the man and placed him in the Garden of Eden, to till it and tend it." Later rabbinic commentary adds detail to God's instructions to Adam: "Look at My works! How beautiful and praiseworthy they are! And everything I made, I created for you. Be careful [though] that you don't spoil or destroy my world—because if you spoil it, there is nobody after you to fix it" (Ecclesiastes *Rabbah* 7:13).

There seems to be more agreement among different faiths on environmental protection than most other issues. In contrast to some of the divisive fundamentalism of recent years, much of the motivation of the faith community's interest in the environment comes from real concern about the world's poor and underprivileged. They are increasingly aware of the disproportionate impact that environmental degradation has in this country and in the world on the poorest people. There are many examples. More intense weather events have dislocated millions. Diversion of grain to make ethanol has increased the price of a meal for the world's poorest, adding millions to those facing starvation worldwide.

The faith community has become a real political force for conservation, especially on the issue of climate change. Their motivation is based in a truly moral response to do better by weak and suffering humans and the other species they hold as part of God's creation. As one of the most powerful forces on earth, their support is essential to success. There is only one other group that might be even more powerful and essential to success—the business community.

6

The Conservation of Business

Power for Change

Ironically, business contains our blessing. It must, because no other institution in the modern world is powerful enough to foster the necessary changes.
—Paul Hawken, *The Ecology of Commerce*

My view is that, if environmentalists aren't willing to engage with big businesses, which are the most powerful forces in the modern world, it won't be possible to solve the world's environmental problems.
—Jared Diamond, *Collapse: How Societies Choose to Fail or Succeed*

THE VOICEMAIL MESSAGE was cryptic, if not menacing. "My name is Herb Smith, and I have been looking into your background. I have learned some interesting things about you, and we need to talk." As a somewhat public figure, executive director of Izaak Walton League of America, bizarre calls to my office were not that unusual. I ignored the voice mail.

Fortunately, Herb called again. At six feet six inches, a former catcher for the Chicago Cubs organization, he was an imposing guy that I would not want to ignore. His genius was executive search, and his task was to find a conservationist willing to serve on the board of a Fortune 500 forest products company involved in a major turnaround in all aspects of corporate performance—but especially environmental compliance. Louisiana-Pacific had fired its CEO, Harry Merlo. They brought in one of the forest and paper industry's most progressive thinkers, Mark Suwyn. Mark wanted an independent environmental presence on the board itself. While executive vice president at International Paper, he had personally witnessed the benefits of the presence of the Conservation Fund chairman Pat Noonan on IP's board. Suwyn had met me as part of the 7th Forest Congress and Sustainable Forestry Initiative and set Herb on the task of due diligence.

Harry Merlo had run LP with an iron fist and lavish lifestyle. Under his leadership, LP had one of corporate America's largest fleets of private jets, sumptuous yachts, and wilderness fishing retreats. Under Merlo, LP was convicted of falsifying emissions data at a plant in Olathe, Colorado. That resulted in a thirty-six-million-dollar fine, sent the plant manager to prison, debarred LP from doing business with the federal government, and required them to put in place an EPA-supervised environmental management system. Under Merlo, LP was accused of falsifying quality data on a siding product by sending a misrepresentative sample for certification. That ended up costing LP one billion dollars in a class action settlement.

Until 1996, when Harry Merlo was fired, LP was one of the most noncompliant forest products companies in the United States. During Merlo's last year alone, LP recorded seventy-six notices of violation of environment regulations. When I was asked to serve on LP's board in 1999, Denis Hayes, founder of Earth Day, wrote to me, "I am astonished, and delighted, that the offer was made. . . . It should be a great learning experience, as well as a chance to help redeem one of the most hated companies in the nation." By 2007, when I cycled off LP's board, LP had no notices of violation and one of the best workplace safety records in any industry. Mark Suwyn had sold the yachts, resorts, and all but two of the corporate jets. He stored extra files in the CEO office hot tub. Over the next few years, he brought sustainability to LP "from the plant manager to the floor sweeper" in the words of one of EPA's most seasoned hard-nosed inspectors, Doug Smith. At the same time

Suwyn somehow found time to chair the board of the Oregon Nature Conservancy. He also returned LP to profitability.

Today, most corporate and business leaders agree that environmental issues are an important part of their businesses. According to a study by McKinsey and Company, 76 percent of executives say that engaging in environmental sustainability contributes positively to shareholder value in the long term. However, only 6 percent say that they have formally embedded this in their business practice, and only 28 percent actively seek opportunities to invest in sustainable practices within their companies.

Most modern executives recognize that responsible environmental practices are good for business and key to corporate reputation. Not only regulators, but customers, investors, and their own employees now expect and demand a certain level of environmental responsibility and performance. There is a new generation of business leadership that has initiated efforts within companies and within entire industries to raise environmental standards. Still, most companies have yet to internalize this as a core business practice, even though they say they recognize the advantages of doing so.

While some progress has been made, there continues to be a large cultural gap between most business and environmental leaders. With examples of shortsighted past practices still fresh in their minds, many environmentalists question whether business really takes environmental issues seriously, as a core value, business issue, marketing opportunity, or even a potential profit center. With more direct engagement and better understanding, both groups could be far more successful and waste far less time on unproductive and wasteful conflicts. After all, conservation is inherently a fundamental business practice. It seeks to maximize return on the investment of a natural asset, while minimizing the depreciation of natural capital. There are a number of steps both sides could take, starting with improving understanding by putting leaders on each other's boards.

Most companies would not think of trying to accomplish their duty of care to oversee company operations without having corporate board director expertise in all major functional areas: compensation practices, legal compliance, human resources, finance and accounting, and the technical aspects of their particular trade. If environment is truly a big part of business, why not have an environmental director as well? As with any other director, all a conservationist wants to do is to help the company make better decisions.

A basic tenet of social psychology is that proximity reduces prejudice. In 1999, when LP's shareholders and directors asked me to serve on their company's board of directors, I was executive director of the Izaak Walton League of America, a national conservation organization that had locked horns with this company and their industry for decades. It was a venture into uncharted territory for both the company and me, but it has the potential to set an innovative precedent— one that every company with significant involvement with natural resources and environmental issues should consider.

If it became a widespread practice, this innovation could provide substantial advantages to companies interested not in window dressing but in the perspective a responsible conservation voice can bring to corporate decision making in an increasingly environment-oriented marketplace. In the areas of product development, marketing, and environmental compliance, for instance, early identification of trends can yield significant improvements in efficiency and substantial competitive advantages. For conservationists, there are similar advantages. The sooner we get an issue on the corporate radar screen, the better our chances are of reducing resistance and securing a durable change in outdated, inefficient, or environmentally destructive practices.

Putting conservationists in the boardroom could also give environmental interests a better understanding of the difficult decisions and tradeoffs faced by businesses presented with complicated and often contradictory demands of their regulators, shareholders, and customers.

After all, the free enterprise system benefits most Americans. Countries with failed economies are the worst for the environment. Even better, maybe we can avoid some of the "train wrecks" and mistrust and divisiveness of the past or find some innovative, win-win solutions to some of the many problems we have historically fought over. The adversarial approach to environmental issues always yields an unstable outcome for everyone—your opponent lives to fight another day. Too often, past environmental conflicts have been characterized more by polemics or political posturing than problem solving—by both sides. The collaborative approach, when genuine, can yield solutions that are more permanent simply because they have the support of more stakeholders.

Jim Nokes, a retired executive vice president from Conoco Philips and a longtime board member and supporter of the Yellowstone Park Foundation, tells me, "When I was in the oil industry, it seemed we tended to adopt extreme positions to counter the extreme proposals coming from the other side. And as you know, that is not a very productive approach. I do think that pragmatic progress is being held captive by extreme positions on both sides."

One of the most pleasant aspects of serving on a company board was the overwhelmingly positive response of company employees who, down the line, told me that they want their company to be as environmentally sound as possible. They were delighted to see this perspective brought in at the board level. My wife heard this even more often than I did, from board and senior executive spouses at company events. We conservationists like to trumpet the fact that in poll after poll 85 percent of the US public support conservation. We sometimes fail to remember that this figure includes millions of corporate employees, their contractors, and shareholders.

There is evidence that some of corporate America already is searching for better advice and less confrontation. Nonprofit executives are more likely than ever to appear on corporate boards. In recent years, the academic-nonprofit community was the second largest source of newly added directors for S&P 500 companies. For their part, some moderate environmental organizations have been bringing business and corporate people onto their boards for many years.

I am one of a handful of conservation leaders to have served on the board of a major public company. I know of four conservation colleagues who have also served, two of whom also had stints in government. I think all have been very positive experiences for both sides.

- William K. Reilly: former CEO, World Wildlife Fund; former administrator, US EPA; director, Conoco Philips; director, DuPont; director, Royal Caribbean International.
- Kathryn S. Fuller: former CEO, World Wildlife Fund; director, Alcoa.
- Patrick F. Noonan: former CEO, The Nature Conservancy; founder and chairman, The Conservation Fund; former director, International Paper; former director, Ashland, Inc.; director, Saul Centers.
- John F. Turner: former director, US Fish and Wildlife Service; former president, The Conservation Fund; former US assistant secretary of state; director, International Paper; director, Ashland Inc.; director, Peabody Energy Company; director, American Electric Power.

Within the radical wing of the environmental community, this practice is viewed skeptically, or even hostilely, by some. There is some risk for those environmentalists who are willing to engage with business. Increasingly, however, engagement with business at this level is viewed as a breakthrough and a standard we should look at for all companies that claim to be environmentally conscientious.

When I agreed to serve on Louisiana Pacific's board early in 1999, I was about to become chair of the "Green Group"—the leadership council of the thirty-five major national environmental group CEOs.

My decision to serve on a corporate board led a couple of environmental group leaders to vigorously oppose my ascending to the chairmanship, but the majority of the group still supported me. Other midlevel environmental leaders wanted to publicly condemn me as an "Uncle Tom." When the sitting Green Group chair pointed out that labor unions and other interest groups had found success by engaging with the corporate world at this level, the debate subsided, but it never went away. My willingness to accept an invitation to influence the direction of a major corporation from a seat on its board led a few Izaak Walton League members to forcefully call for my resignation as executive director—a call they repeated for the next eight years. All but one of the Izaak Walton League board supported this outreach, so the calls for my resignation were never acted on, but this type of outreach has its downside to a career.

Putting a conservationist on a corporate board to green-wash a company's image, rather than to help it make better decisions, would be a mistake for both parties. My experience was very positive. During almost nine years with LP, 1999–2007, we returned the company to profitability and doubled the stock price while reducing environmental notices of violation from 76 to 0. LP divested holdings in the redwood forests of California, closed their operations in southeast Alaska's old-growth forests, and focused their business on high-tech engineered wood products that do not require old growth and can use smaller short-rotation trees from thinning projects and sustainable forestry. They put in place an environmental management system that saved the company $18 million in 2003. This alone added $0.17 to the company's earnings per share for that year.

A conservation perspective can help the bottom line for business. Too often in the past, we have traded short-term gains in income for permanent losses in wealth. Real long-term wealth is created not by how fast we use our natural assets but by how well we use them. The world's long-term economic future is inextricably linked to efficiency, to the return on resources we attain rather than the speed at which we use them. "Exhaust America First" should not be our policy for natural resource use.

Pres. Theodore Roosevelt understood this over a century ago: "I recognize the right and duty of this generation to develop and use the natural resources of our land: but I do not recognize the right to waste them, or to rob, by wasteful use, the generations who come after us. The nation behaves well if it treats the natural resources as assets, which it must turn over to the next generation increased and not impaired in value. . . . The conservation of natural resources is the fundamental problem. Unless we solve that problem, it will avail us little to solve all others."

Clearly, putting a conservationist on a corporate board will not, in itself, solve anything. But if proximity does indeed reduce prejudice, it might just save business billions in unnecessary litigation, public relations, political contributions, and other essentially unproductive uses of limited capital that could be better invested elsewhere. I look at engagement at the board level as a great opportunity for cross-cultural understanding, much like the exchanges that go on between nations through the State Department, Rotary International, or the American Field Service.

During my term on Louisiana Pacific's board, I estimate that I had detailed positive personal conversations with at least one thousand people about the experience. Many of these people were "thought leaders" in the natural resources and conservation field. I gave speeches to groups that included at least another ten thousand and wrote articles available to about another one million people. What if just one hundred of the top companies that have significant exposure to environmental issues were to add just one responsible conservationist to their boards? What would the multiplier effect be on understanding the conflicting demands that these businesses face from customers, regulators, shareholders, Wall Street analysts, employees, and the media? How would this enhanced understanding help not just on environmental issues but on business sustainability overall? What "teachable moments" would both groups enjoy? Would we find more creative solutions rather than creative sound bites attacking the other side?

Germany's economy is the world's strongest, with the lowest unemployment rate. Their system of "co-determination" puts union members, environmentalists, and other potential adversaries on corporate boards. The experience gives these "adversary ambassadors" a firsthand view of the tough decisions and tradeoffs that must be made by corporate boards while humanizing both sides.

Economic progress and environmental quality are irrevocably linked. If we consider the costly battles of the past and the uncertainty brought on by the current stalemate on environmental policymaking, a world where every corporate board with environmental exposure included a responsible conservation leader might be a better place for all. Peter Drucker, the famed management consultant and "social ecologist" wrote, "If the managers of our major institutions, and especially of business, do not take responsibility for the common good, no one else can or will."

About a year into my tenure on LP's board, I had an epiphany that now seems so obvious to me it is embarrassing. From the beginning, I had wondered why several of my board colleagues would give 5–6 weekends per year, many evening conference calls, and the personal liability exposure that goes with serving on a company board. These highly successful executives were insanely busy and had their own major companies to run. It certainly was not the money. In their world, the board compensation was pretty insignificant. Then it came to me. They served for the same reason that the board members of my Izaak Walton League or any other nonprofit board member would serve. They wanted to make the world a better place. An efficient and ethical free enterprise system is a greater good for all.

Business and conservation interests can do better by working together than they have done by working apart. Conscientious engagement at the board level would provide a good place to start. We all share a predominant interest in a healthy economy and a healthy environment. With real engagement, we could avoid some of the unproductive conflicts of the past, such as "the war in the woods" between the forest products industry and the environmental community.

7

The War in the Woods

Tough Love between Tree Huggers and Timber Beasts

Deforestation was a, or the, major factor in all the collapses
of past societies described in this book.
—Jared Diamond, *Collapse: How Societies Choose to Fail or Succeed*

Being an agent of change is gratifying only in retrospect.
—John Heissenbuttel, former executive,
American Forest and Paper Association

THE FACT THAT THE ENVIRONMENTALISTS are pejoratively called
"tree huggers" and the forest products employees are called "timber beasts" should be the first clue of the deep-seated, historic hostil-
ity between forest products businesses and some of the environmental
community. For decades, the two warring factions have fought each
other to a stalemate on a number of issues. Ironically, at times both
sides have done so in direct conflict with their own core interests and
oft-stated objectives. To best protect from irresponsible timber harvest
here and abroad, to provide a stable business environment, and to assure a reliable supply of domestic wood and rural jobs, they need each
other. They should be allies behind a vision of sustainable forestry in
the United States. With some listening and a little compromise from
both sides, they could be.

Any discussion of forestry in the United States needs to start with recognition of two basic axioms. We use a lot of forest products, and we have a high dependence on foreign sources for wood—even higher than we do oil—about 75 percent of our demand. When we do not harvest sustainably in the United States, we inevitably fill that demand with wood products from nations with lower environmental standards than ours. When a timber harvest is stopped in the United States, it does not necessarily prevent environmental impacts—it exports them and usually exacerbates them. We also lose jobs at home and contribute to our foreign trade deficit. Today, timber harvest on national forests has virtually come to a halt, increasing demand from foreign sources.

Most professional foresters and timber company executives readily acknowledge that the past forest management practices in the United States, Canada, and much of the rest of the world were unsustainable. Trees were dealt with as a crop to be harvested. The US Forest Service is still part of the Department of Agriculture rather than the Department of the Interior with the three other major land management agencies: the National Park Service, US Fish and Wildlife Service, and Bureau of Land Management. There was little thought of the impact of clear-cuts to water quality and wildlife and little regard for the impact of timber harvest to other values, such as recreation and tourism. Clear-cuts on steep slopes where no trees or streamside buffers were left have caused extensive damage to entire ecosystems. Today, old-growth forests, with their unique and cherished ecosystems, exist in only a few remnants. Damage to fisheries was widespread. Some runs were wiped out entirely, either by erosion, increased water temperature from streamside logging, or the deposits of sawmill residue and bark into the waterways. In the Northwest, magnificent runs of native salmon are all but gone, the once staggering abundance now replaced by Endangered Species Act protection.

Today, forestry practices have come a long way. Many practices that were acceptable just twenty years ago are not acceptable today.

Restoration is occurring on land poorly harvested years ago. As is often the case, change to modern practices did not come easily. Industry fought many of the advanced silvicultural practices they now endorse as modern forestry today. Still, change has come, and most environmentalists would agree that forest practices are light-years ahead of where they were just a decade or two ago.

In the early 1970s, West Virginia sportsmen with the Izaak Walton League filed a lawsuit on the Monongahela National Forest, where massive clear-cuts and the resulting erosion were having a devastating impact on fish and wildlife. Their lawsuit, *Izaak Walton League v. Agriculture Secretary Earl Butz,* succeeded beyond their wildest dreams. The court found that many timber practices commonly used, such as massive clear-cutting, were illegal. The decision shut down forestry in several mid-Atlantic states and threatened to halt logging nationwide.

In response to the court's decision, in 1976 Congress quickly passed the National Forest Management Act. The act invalidated many common timber practices, required that a detailed guidance be established for forest plans, and ordered a stop to large-scale clear-cuts. Like most legislation, this act took years for implementation—rules to be drafted, commented on, amended, accepted, oftentimes litigated, and then enforced. Throughout the 1980s, timber harvest on the national forests remained high, peaking at twelve billion board feet (one square foot one inch thick) per year. Many poor practices were slowly eliminated. By 1995, harvest was down to two billion board feet, which was arguably too low. Demand would be met by foreign sources with standards lower than ours.

CLINTON'S ROADLESS RULE

By 1992, most of the readily available national forest timber had been cut. Cutting timber on national forests now required expensive new roads, higher costs, and greater environmental impact. The federal government subsidized cuts in areas too remote to be cost-effectively harvested. Below-cost timber sales became unpopular with the public and Congress. Timber harvest fell precipitously, but that did not stop the war between the forest industry and environmentalists on the management of fifty-seven million acres of roadless national forest lands.

In 1964, Congress passed and the president signed the Wilderness Act. It defines wilderness as: "A wilderness, in contrast with those areas where man and his own works dominate the landscape, is hereby recognized as an area where the earth and community of life are untrammeled by man, where man himself is a visitor who does not remain." The act created a new level of protection for public land but protected just a tiny amount of land that qualified under the new law. Congress set aside only nine million acres of public land—an area equal to about one-tenth the size of the state of Montana. In these "designated Wilderness areas," all motorized use is prohibited, but hunting, fishing, grazing and even mining is still allowed in most cases. The Wilderness Act does not add more public land. Its designation is a protective overlay on existing federal land, providing the highest level of protection possible. It protected only a fraction of the two hundred million acres that had never been developed and qualified for this level of protection. The Wilderness Act was a compromise. The act was also a first step toward building a much larger system of public land protection.

In the act, Congress set up a mechanism that requires federal land management agencies to evaluate land that Congress and the president might add to the system. Since the act first passed in 1963, every president has signed legislation adding to the system. Pres. Ronald Reagan signed legislation adding more acreage to this system than any other president. By 2012, the National Wilderness Preservation System included 109 million acres, just under 5 percent of the United States, or an area larger than all of Montana. Wilderness protection is an overlay that can be designed on any federal land. The vast majority of the acreage that is designated "wilderness" is split between four land management agencies: National Park Service—44 million acres; US Forest

The National Wilderness Preservation System includes approximately 109 million acres in 662 protected wilderness areas on four types of lands managed by the US government:

- National forests
- National parks
- National wildlife refuges
- Bureau of Land Management lands

Since the Wilderness Act first passed in 1963, every president has signed legislation adding to the system.

Service—36 million acres; Bureau of Land Management—21 million acres; and US Fish and Wildlife Refuges—7 million acres.

Within the national forests of the lower forty-eight states there are another 58 million acres, an area about equal to the state of Idaho, of what is called inventoried roadless areas (IRA). Much of this land is in the West. These IRAs have wilderness attributes and could qualify for National Wilderness Preservation System protection but have not been included so far. It remains the largest area of unprotected and undisturbed land remaining in the United States. Its protection is a top priority for much of the environmental community. These lands tend to be remote, high elevation, and remained roadless because they have low value for timber and other commodities. They do have increasingly high value for watershed protection, wildlife, and recreation.

After decades of war on this issue, including repeated rounds of roadless area review and evaluation dating back to the 1960s, several knowledgeable people have called for a truce. Jack Ward Thomas, Forest Service chief during President Clinton's first term, observed, "when it comes to U.S Forest Service roadless areas, environmentalists have won the battle, but are out there bayoneting the wounded." Chief Thomas outlined his compromise: protect the roadless areas in exchange for more timber harvest in the parts of the forest that already had a road network and had regrown from earlier timber harvests. Existing roads would make the harvest more cost-effective, and much of the area had been cut many decades earlier resulting in even-age timber that had grown to a point where it needed to be thinned. Other areas were suffering from uncharacteristic outbreaks of tree disease that might benefit from thinning.

More importantly, there was simply much more wood outside the roadless areas. By some estimates, the portion of the national forests that already had a forest road infrastructure could sustainably provide fifty times more wood than would ever be possible from the roadless parts of the forest—where any harvest would be much more expensive. Sustainable harvest in the roaded areas would reduce dependency on foreign sources of wood product, create jobs in rural areas, and help balance the trade deficit. Chief Thomas and his successor during Clinton's second term, Chief Mike Dombeck, both recognized that the roadless areas would not produce much timber and then only at a high cost. These areas were better off being kept in their roadless status where the wildlife, watershed, and recreational values could best be managed.

In fact, Mike Dombeck had planned to implement this type of compromise once the roadless rule protecting these areas that he had championed was in place. He planned to tell the environmental groups that now that their top priority roadless areas were protected, they would need to allow more timber management in other parts of the forest. All of this harvest was intended to be "stewardship cuts" on parts of the national forest that already had roads and a history of timber management. All was to be sustainable harvest designed to meet forest health, wildlife, watershed protection, and fire prevention goals while providing a reliable and steady source of timber and jobs in much of rural America.

Unfortunately, the opportunity to provide more reliable sources of timber and jobs was lost to partisan politics. In 2001, just before leaving office, President Clinton finally issued a rule protecting fifty-eight million acres of US Forest Service roadless land. The rulemaking process had been robust, to say the least. There were two million public comments in favor of his new rule, more than any other public action in history. Support was widespread. There was a lot at stake. More natural land would be protected than by any action in over twenty years. Even groups like conservation giant the Nature Conservancy, which engages in policy issues very carefully, openly supported the roadless rule due to the extensive protection of biological diversity that it would provide.

A few weeks later, just after coming into office, Pres. George W. Bush rescinded the rule. Over the next eight years, there were at least six conflicting legal decisions that literally repealed the repeal of the repeal. It left the overall status of these areas uncertain and gave inconsistent instructions to different regions of our US National Forest Service—making the job of managing these areas almost impossible.

About a year after George W. Bush became president and rescinded Clinton's roadless rule, several of the more moderate conservation-minded sportsmen's groups mounted a collaborative effort to broker a compromise along the lines of what Thomas had proposed years earlier. In late 2002, after more than a year of careful deliberation, these groups—including Trout Unlimited, Izaak Walton League, Wildlife Management Institute, and Theodore Roosevelt Conservation Partnership—took a draft compromise and invited over fifty very diverse groups to meet, respond to the draft compromise, and discuss their ideas. The invitees included a broad array of stakeholders: industry, recreation groups, hunters, rural county commissioners, and environmental groups. Regrettably, nine major environmental groups, including the Sierra Club, Natural Resources Defense Council, and Earthjustice boycotted the meeting. Even worse, they pressured colleague groups who wanted to attend into not coming. Worse still, two junior staff people from the Greater Yellowstone Coalition sent sarcastic and personally demeaning emails to some of the sportsmen group leaders for their audacity at suggesting a compromise.

The effort to protect US Forest Service roadless areas is another powerful example of the disconnect between these natural allies. Roads can hurt hunting and fishing by fragmenting habitat and increasing runoff. So why were many sporting groups silent or even opposed to a 2000 rule to protect these areas? One reason was because there was a lack of outreach to sportsmen when the proposed rule was developed. Environmentalists felt they had the ear of President Clinton and Vice President Gore so they did not need to listen to sportsmen or to include their ideas in the proposed rule. When President Bush came to office, environmental groups still did not come to sportsmen to see what kind of compromise they would support.

Ironically, only seven miles of new roads were built in our national forests during the eight years of the Bush administration, causing some to question what exactly this fight is about.

HEALTHY FORESTS?

In the name of "healthy forests" a second war in the woods was fought in the Bush administration—despite almost complete bipartisan agreement on the goal of reducing fire risk. After a record fire season in the West in the summer of 2000, the western governors and the Clinton administration agreed that there needed to be significantly more forest management and more tree thinning throughout the West. There was virtual consensus on this point, especially in areas termed the Wildlife Urban Interface, that area where the national forest borders towns and people's homes. What was needed was the money to do the job.

Instead of appropriating the needed funds for the forest management that all the leaders had agreed to, this became a political issue. Progress on the ground came to a halt. For the next three years, 2001–2003, the Bush administration and Congress fought a protracted leg-

islative battle involving the Healthy Forest Restoration Act over doing what they had already agreed to do. During that time, there was
little new funding for forest management and little acceleration of the
actual forest health work that needed to be done. The Healthy Forest
Restoration Act passed in 2003 but added little to the existing authority needed to manage the national forests and even less new money
for real work on the ground. Finger pointing over the legislation was a
distraction that drew people's attention away from the fact that nothing was being done.

Three years were lost. What was really needed—a federal appropriation equal to the task of thinning forests in the Wildlife Urban
Interface—was not done. Unnaturally hot fires continued to burn the
West. Fighting those fires now eats up an increasing percentage of already decimated Forest Service budgets, which has led to the elimination of many programs that would prevent fires. Only a tiny fraction
of the preventive measures that were agreed to by the Clinton administration and the western governors back in 2000 were implemented.

BUSH'S ROADLESS RULE

In 2004, the Bush administration took up the issue of the nation's
roadless forestland. Soon after coming to office, they had rescinded the
rule promulgated by the Clinton administration. In 2004, they put forward a new rule that took a state-by-state approach to roadless area
protection. States could petition to write their own rule to govern the
use of these public lands owned by the federal government. The administration chartered and appointed a thirteen-member citizen group
under the Federal Advisory Committee Act. The panel would review
petitions from state governments on how they would like these federal
lands within their states to be managed and administered and make
recommendations to the secretary of agriculture. The group was called
the Roadless Area Conservation National Advisory Committee, or

RACNAC. It was a very diverse group and started its work with much promise. I was one of the thirteen members.

The first five states to present petitions, including two with Republican governors, chose to go with levels of protection basically indistinguishable from the 2000 Roadless Rule put together by the Clinton administration. Years later, after a loss of faith in the process, none of these states chose to go forward with a rulemaking process. Several other states chose to bypass the process altogether. Frustrated by decades of gridlock on this issue, they deferred to a series of lawsuits that were pending. In the case of California, they chose not to participate due to a clearly stated distrust of the Bush administration.

The only states to take full advantage of the process and take it to a legal conclusion were Idaho and Colorado. The initial Idaho petition was a visionary compromise and could have set an example for the rest of the nation. It was presented to the RACNAC by then Idaho Lt. Gov. Jim Risch, who was elected to the US Senate in 2008. Idaho's original petition proposed to give 95 percent of Idaho's inventoried roadless areas a level of protection equal to or better than the 2000 rule. It was hailed by the RACNAC and even skeptically endorsed by the environmental groups who bird-dogged the process.

Unfortunately, when Idaho's actual proposed rule came out, it bore little resemblance to their visionary petition. Safeguards for thousands of acres had disappeared, and rules for governing the use of off-highway vehicles in these areas would not be considered. Worse, the RACNAC's support for the terms of the initial petition was misrepresented by the state of Idaho as support for the proposed rule that came out over a year later. This put all of the conservation organization members of the RACNAC in a very difficult position. We were already under a great deal of pressure from some environmentalists who were inherently suspicious of the whole process. Before we had ever seen the proposed rule, the public was told in a film clip featuring

Governor Risch that the members of the RACNAC enthusiastically supported it. The state of Idaho staff, who were aware of the mistake, showed the film to audiences around the state without acknowledging the error.

The loss of trust that ensued crippled the process, which had started with such great promise. It ended up with committee members back in their interest group corners rehashing the roadless area arguments of the past forty years. The off-road vehicle users groups refused to compromise at all. Much of the forest products industry goes along with the off-road groups, even though there is little compelling business interest in doing so. It is hard to see how joining forces with off-road users is in the best interests of industry shareholders if it impairs compromise that might open more domestic harvest. Several of us began to wonder if the process was a valid use of our time, but we hung in there.

After more months of process plagued with difficulties, a compromise emerged that protected much of the roadless national forest in Idaho. It fell short of what it could have been and did less for conservation than the visionary petition originally presented by Sen. Jim Risch. It did far less for forest health, sustainable forestry, and local jobs than the compromise envisioned by the two previous US Forest Service chiefs, Jack Thomas and Mike Dombeck. The compromise was acceptable to moderate groups like Trout Unlimited, the Idaho Conservation League, and the Theodore Roosevelt Conservation Partnership. The Greater Yellowstone Coalition has sued to overturn it. They had never participated in the compromise process despite several personal invitations to do so.

The roadless area issue has been cussed and discussed for forty-five years. In 2009, Pres. Barack Obama's new agriculture secretary, Tom Vilsack, called for a time out, whereby no new roads could be built for a year while he decided what to do with the whole mess. In 2012, Colorado's compromise rule was approved, and the US Supreme Court refused to hear an appeal asking the court to strike down the Clinton roadless rule. For now, it remains the law of the US Forest Service land. The war in the woods continues.

FOREST CERTIFICATION

The United States is more dependent on foreign sources of wood than we are on foreign oil. One of the outcomes of the 1992 United Nation's Conference on Environment and Development, the Rio Earth Summit, was recognition that the pace and practice of forestry worldwide was dangerously unsustainable. At the time, great attention was being given to the loss of tropical rainforests, but harvest practices in temperate forests were of significant concern as well. Unfortunately, the intergovernmental process had failed to produce an international forest compact to address the problem. This led a number of major environmental foundations and conservation organizations to come together and found the Forest Stewardship Council to begin a process for certification of sustainable forestry practices worldwide.

In principle, forest certification requires that producers of wood products who meet a set of standards would be able to certify their product as sustainably produced and identify it as such with a product label. This market-driven approach would give consumers the chance to buy a product they could feel good about and would, hopefully, drive the forest products industry to better management practices overall. The idea had a lot of appeal, but once again environmentalists and the forest products industry could not find common ground. At the first General Assembly of the Forest Stewardship Council, the major forest products companies were not invited. At least that is how the companies tell the story. So, the major companies started their own certification system, the Sustainable Forestry Initiative (SFI). These two very similar programs have been at war ever since.

From the beginning, large retailers of forest products welcomed certification as a value-added marketing tool. Their interest drove a lot of the program development. Arthur Blank, the co-founder, CFO, then CEO of Home Depot was particularly visionary. As the largest retailer of forest products, his interest alone drove much of the certification effort, particularly from the major companies and their trade association—the American Forest and Paper Association (AF&PA). For years, Blank was the ghost in the room during meetings developing the Sustainable Forestry Initiative—the unseen presence in scores of meetings driving an entire industry toward environmentally sustainable practices. I attended many of those meetings.

In 1995, AF&PA president Henson Moore asked me to serve on a panel of outside experts who were advising the industry group on the development of the Sustainable Forestry Initiative. I found myself among a very knowledgeable, diverse, and experienced group that included two former US Forest Service chiefs—Max Peterson and Jack Ward Thomas—and the deputy chief at the time—Phil Janik. Also included were several state foresters, the executive vice president of the Society of American Foresters, a couple of distinguished university professors and one of America's most innovative conservation leaders, Patrick Noonan, chairman of the Conservation Fund. From 1996 to 2000 I chaired this committee, the Sustainable Forestry Initiative's External Review Panel.

Over the next six years, by engaging with the forest products community, we were able to help move an entire industry toward more sustainable practices. With the help of two conservation-minded foresters that I supervised, audits were conducted at over seventy company sites. We documented exemplary practices publicly, and privately offered the first notice of areas where improvement was needed privately, and followed up to see that the issues were resolved. Generally, we found that timber management on company-owned land was good and often excellent. Procured wood—wood brought to mills by independent contractors—was much more difficult to certify as sustainably harvested.

Due primarily to tax law changes that required public companies that held their own land to pay at least twice the tax as other holding companies, most forest products companies divested of much of their land holdings between 2000 and 2003. Land holdings of the major public companies were sold to privately held timber management organizations or real estate investment trusts. Since these were usually not public companies that were openly accountable to shareholders and the Securities Exchange Commission, it became much harder to monitor timber practices. The reduced level of disclosure required of the privately held companies made "chain of custody" determinations, whereby the source of wood for various products is tracked to assure it was sustainably grown and harvested, much more difficult.

Logically, consumers would be better served by one coordinated certification standard in the marketplace. The diverse members of the SFI External Review Panel were able to arrange meetings between the leadership of the two approaches, the Forest Stewardship Council and Sustainable Forestry Initiative. We were never able to bring them together. Today, these two very similar forest product certification systems operate separately, creating confusion in the marketplace, duplication of effort, and more cost for all. SFI claims that certification competition is good, but there is no doubt that both camps would better serve forest products consumers and the forests themselves by a unified approach.

What is most ironic about the ongoing war in the woods? The fact that the one time when the warring factions all spent a few days together, they found that there was widespread agreement on a common set of principles. There have been eight Forest Congresses held in the United States, starting in 1882, when the first Forest Congress was held. Other Forest Congresses were held in 1905, 1946, 1953, 1963, 1975, and 1996. The US Forest Service, to mark their 100th anniversary, held a special Centennial Forest Congress in 2005.

I was a senior sponsor of the Seventh Forest Congress, held in Washington, DC, in 1996. It was the largest and most diverse of all the forest conferences, with over fifteen hundred participants. Forest company executives, academics, professional foresters, small landowners, environmentalists, county commissioners, off-road vehicle users, and "wise use" groups that opposed the very existence of public lands were all present. Included were radical factions from both sides. During one of the group census polls, 20 percent of those present did not agree with the statement that "conflicts over forest issues will be resolved through nonviolent processes." This was a diverse gathering.

What they did agree on, by 90 percent margins or higher, was breathtaking:

- Long-term sustainable management was needed to provide a range of ecological, economic, and social benefits;
- Mixed public and private ownership was beneficial;
- Public interests exist on private land, and private owners have a responsibility for stewardship that should be respected; and
- Sound science should guide management, reforestation, and restoration, which should be a top priority on all forests.

Essentially, these natural allies agreed on how to manage the nation's forests, both public and private. They agreed that we do not need to "lock up" all public lands but that designated wilderness was appropriate in some cases. We need to respect private land and provide an economic return of forestland is in the public interest. Unfortunately, this consensus never resulted in a breakthrough in enlightened forest policy. The necessary long-term engagement and compromise never occurred. So far, the war in the woods continues between these natural allies—who care about our national forests and fundamentally share a basic vision of forest management in the United States, but spend most of their time with their own kind rather than in problem-solving outreach that leads to success.

8
Natural Allies

Environmentalists, Hunters and Anglers, and Rural Residents

There are some who can live without wild things, and some who cannot.
—Aldo Leopold, *A Sand County Almanac*

The best decisions come from a diversity of opinion.
—Benjamin Franklin

SUPPORT FOR CONSERVATION is widespread. For years, public opinion polls have shown that an overwhelming percentage of Americans favor sound conservation of natural resources and the environment. A 2012 national survey of voters conducted by the bipartisan research team of Fairbank, Maslin, Maullin, Metz & Associates (D) and Public Opinion Strategies (R) found overwhelming majorities of Americans of all political persuasions believe that "conserving the country's natural resources—land, air and water—is patriotic. From Tea Party Republicans to liberal Democrats, four out of five Americans agreed with this statement. They also believe we can protect land and water and have a strong economy at the same time, while only 16 percent believe that those concerns are even "sometimes" in conflict. Other nations have found similar results. This includes strong majorities across all major demographic categories: ethnic, religious, racial, age, gender and political party affiliation.

Logically, support is often strongest among those who spend the most time outdoors. Most hunters and anglers, and many rural residents, have special bonds to nature and the outdoors. Unfortunately, these conservationists usually do not have good relations with the environmentalists. On the rare occasion when these groups do come together, the benefits for conservation are amazing.

CONSERVATION ORGANIZATIONS AND THEIR HISTORY

Earth Day 1970 is often held out as the birth of environmentalism, but during the first seventy years of the twentieth century, prior to Earth Day, a great deal of conservation was accomplished. Some of today's leading conservation groups have more history prior to Earth Day than they do since. The Sierra Club was founded in 1892, National Audubon Society in 1905, the Wildlife Management Institute in 1911, the Izaak Walton League in 1922, and Ducks Unlimited in 1938. For many Americans, conservation had been a primary cause and passion for many generations prior to Earth Day. The cultural revolution of the 1960s and 70s did not discover the environment. To the extent that it associated conservation with counterculture causes and changed public perception of what had been a mainstream issue since the late 1800s, Earth Day may not have even helped the cause.

In fact, the greatest era for conservation may have been at the turn of the twentieth century. Those years heralded a remarkable framework of new laws—breathtaking in scope and unlike anything the world had ever seen. More land was protected than at any time in history, and several laws were put in place that set precedents and continue to be in use today. These include the Forest Resource Act of 1894, the Lacey Act of 1900, and the Antiquities Act of 1906. Pres. Theodore Roosevelt used the Forest Resource Act to create 159 forest reserves totaling 150 million acres—still the most land set aside at any one time in human history. During his last year in office, Roosevelt also held the most remarkable conservation meeting in history, the Governor's Conference on Natural Resources. In attendance were forty-four out of forty-six state governors and hundreds of other experts. No conservation meeting like this has been held in the years since Roosevelt's epic 1908 gathering.

In 1906, President Roosevelt persuaded Congress to pass the Antiquities Act, which allows the president to establish national monuments by executive order. National monuments are protected areas, like national parks, but with less protection and usually less funding. With this one act, he put in place a law that all but three of the presidents that followed him used to protect more land and water than any other single law in US history. Roosevelt immediately used the Antiquities Act to protect the Devil's Tower and the Grand Canyon. Since that time, the act has been used over one hundred times by fifteen presidents to protect natural, historic, and cultural treasures. Only Presidents Richard Nixon, Ronald Reagan, and George H. W. Bush did not use this act. Many of these monuments have become national parks, including Grand Canyon, Bryce, Zion, and Acadia National Parks. Pres. Bill Clinton used the act in 1996 to establish the 1.9-million-acre Escalante Grand Staircase National Monument. By comparison, Yellowstone National Park is 2.2 million acres. In a sense, Pres. George W. Bush used the Antiquities Act to protect the most acreage of all, 145 million acres of ocean, reefs, islands, and atolls to the north, west, and south of Hawaii. When President Bush created the Papahanaumokuakea Marine National Monument in 2006 and the Pacific Remote Islands National Monument in 2007, he used the Antiquities Act to protect more area than any other president. He followed an initiative started by Theodore Roosevelt, who created Hawaiian Islands National Wildlife Refuge in 1909.

THE HISTORY OF MISUNDERSTANDING

Most of conservation's early gains were won by men and women who hunted and fished, such as Theodore Roosevelt. Today, strong majorities of Americans still support them—even if they do not participate themselves. Only about fifteen million Americans hunt each year, about 6 percent of the adult population, though eighteen million self-identify as hunters. About fifty million people fish, about 17 percent of the total population. Almost everyone supports fishing, and 80 percent of the general public support legal hunting. The key word here is legal. A majority of Americans feel that a lot of hunters violate laws or practice unsafe behavior while hunting. About half of those who hunt agree with this perception. The greatest threat to the future of hunting comes from the slob hunters within the hunting community itself rather than the small minority of Americans who are anti-hunting.

Sportsmen and environmentalists have much in common and much to offer each other. Both spend a great deal of time outdoors in wild places where the rules of nature still predominate. They share an intimate understanding and great love of the outdoors. They know the inspiration and even ecstasy of special experiences the outdoors provides that seem to come out of nowhere. Unlike most Americans, these are all people who would rather be in the field, on a river, or in the woods than in a shopping mall, sports arena, or home watching television. Even though they enjoy the wild places in different ways, they remain the two groups in our society who spend the most time outdoors.

Neither group, environmentalists or sportsmen, is large enough to protect wildlife habitat and wild places alone. They need each other. Roughly four million of those who hunt and fish belong to an organization that promotes conservation. Roughly the same number of Americans, about four million, belongs to a national environmental group. This is about 2 percent of the adult public for each group. While there are also a great many local conservation groups, about ten thousand total, this is not a large enough constituency to have overwhelming impact. There is some overlap in membership between sportsmen and environmental groups but not much. Membership in both groups is declining, with more declines likely in the future due to age demographics. Based on reliable polling data, the average age of members in both organized environmental groups and hunting and angling conservation groups is about fifty-seven years old—far older than the average age of Americans.

The Green Group is the forum of CEOs of the major national environmental groups. I was a member from 1995 to 2007 and its chair from 1999 to 2000. In 1999, most of these environmental groups took the remarkable step of creating a combined database of all the names of the members of all their groups. The effort was managed by a new organization, blandly named by intent as the Partnership Project, with the board made up of representatives from the participating groups. They started a coalition web site called saveourenvironment.org. I was a founding board member. Since groups like this are cooperators on mission but competitors for members, media, and money, nonprofit "trade associations" like this can be a curse to manage. Fortunately, this group hired a smart, young, and savvy woman named Julie Waterman. A marathoner and Iron Man race competitor, Julie had coordinated the Green Group for eight years. She was the right person for the job. Since 2000, this group has seamlessly helped coordinate the environmental community's outreach for a decade, keeping below the radar of the public media.

For nonprofit organizations, member names are a group's clientele, their "stock in trade," so they jealousy guard their members' contact information. The Partnership Project's combined list was created with strict rules for its use and with iron-clad agreements to guard its confidentiality. The groups started the Partnership Project to enhance ef-

GREEN GROUP

These national environmental groups have a combined membership of around four million members.

- American Rivers
- Apollo Alliance
- Center for International Environmental Law
- Clean Water Action
- Defenders of Wildlife
- Earthjustice
- Environment America
- Environmental Defense Fund
- Friends of the Earth
- Greenpeace
- Izaak Walton League
- Land Trust Alliance
- League of Conservation Voters
- National Audubon Society
- National Parks Conservation Association
- National Religious Partnership for the Environment
- National Tribal Environmental Council
- National Wildlife Foundation
- Native American Rights Fund
- Population Action International
- The Wilderness Society
- Natural Resources Defense Council
- Oceana
- Ocean Conservancy
- Pew Environmental Group
- Physicians for Social Responsibility
- Population Connection
- Rails to Trails Conservancy
- Sierra Club
- The Trust for Public Land
- Union of Concerned Scientists
- World Resources Institute
- World Wildlife Fund

ficiency and to eliminate duplicative effort, primarily to prevent several groups from sending a similar call to action on the same issue to the same activist.

There is a third type of group of conservationists who are focused primarily on land conservation. These groups are the newest arrivals on the conservation scene and in many ways the most successful. They include the largest conservation group in the world, the Nature Conservancy, and the smallest local land trusts of just a few members. The

LAND PROTECTION ORGANIZATIONS

There are approximately seventeen hundred local land trusts working to protect open space and wildlife habitat. Most of them are part of the Land Trust Alliance. The largest of these groups, and the largest conservation group in the world, is the Nature Conservancy.

total membership of the land trust community is about two million, and is growing.

The more enlightened members of the hunting-angling, land conservation, and environmental groups all hold Aldo Leopold's classic book *A Sand County Almanac* in great esteem. The first sentence of the book describes most of the groups' supporters: "There are some who can live without wild things, and some who cannot." Leaders from these groups give literally billions of dollars and millions of hours to conservation, but the types of groups tend to be organized much differently.

Most environmental groups are generalists that work on a large range of issues, with much overlap with colleague groups. The Sierra Club, Environmental Defense, Natural Resources Defense Council, World Resources Institute, Greenpeace, Friends of the Earth, and the Izaak Walton League all work on a broad range of conservation issues. Defenders of Wildlife, National Wildlife Foundation, and World Wildlife Fund focus on all wildlife issues—broadly defined. National Audubon is dedicated to birds and their habitat but has a great commitment to a network of nature centers and much else. Other groups focus on oceans, national parks, human population issues, or land conservation. One group, Earthjustice, is, effectively, the law firm for the environmental movement. Another, the League of Conservation Voters, is the political and electoral center—though some groups also have their own political action committees. Environmentalists are more likely to lean Democrat than Republican, but there are important exceptions. Curiously, there is no regular gathering of the environmental groups, as there is for wildlife conservation sportsmen, the land trusts, and most other nonprofit sector organizations. Most commercial trade associations, governmental entities like counties and governors, educators, and most causes have annual gatherings, but not environmentalists. Many groups hold their own meetings, but the environmental community is almost unique in that there is not a mass gathering where representatives of all the groups come together.

Many environmental groups are supported by very dedicated volunteers who have a hand in setting organizational policy. Logically, the most passionate people are the biggest financial supporters. This can make it difficult for professional staff to support essential compromise, even when they think it is smart strategy. No one in a mission-driven field like conservation wants to be known as the great compromiser, and some wealthy board members will not tolerate it. A few groups have a robust policy-setting process for citizen members, but professional staff or even organizational donors set most environmental group policies. This tends to put group leadership out of step with everyday American pragmatism.

You might not agree with their decisions, but when the Sierra Club, Izaak Walton League, or National Wildlife Federation take a public position, those positions have been set by rank-and-file members through a tedious stakeholder process. Most other groups have it a bit easier. Their members vote with their checkbooks, leaving policy-making to the professional staff. Some groups, such as the Pew Environment Group and the Center for Biological Diversity, do not represent a membership base that sets policy and are not really accountable to anyone. They are usually funded by a few major donors or foundations. Some of them generate a great deal of press, or file a lot of lawsuits, but what does it really mean when they take a position? Who do they really represent? This phenomenon is seen with some of the anti-environmental groups on the right wing, as well, and presents an obstacle to durable progress from both sides.

In contrast to the generalist-tending environmental groups, hunter and angler conservation groups tend to be much more focused. Many groups focus on a only a single species, such as the Rocky Mountain Elk Foundation, Pheasants Forever, the Ruffed Grouse Society, Whitetails Unlimited, National Wild Turkey Federation, or Mule Deer Foundation. Others focus on a family of species, such as Ducks Unlimited, Quail Unlimited, or Trout Unlimited. Only a few groups—the Wildlife Management Institute, Boone and Crockett Club, Izaak Walton League, and Theodore Roosevelt Conservation Alliance—have a broad agenda. Since 1920, much of the hunting and angling conservation community groups have met annually with state, government, and university leaders at the North American Wildlife and Natural Resources Conference. In 2000, many of the leading nonprofit hunting conservation groups organized a leadership council to better coordinate their work. It is called the American Wildlife Conservation Partners. I was a founding member of this group.

Like most trade associations in business or nonprofit works, environmental and hunting and angling conservation groups suffer from their more radical members polarizing issues unnecessarily. This dynamic is not unlike what we see in the Middle East and almost everywhere there is armed conflict, where the atrocities of the most radical factions make it very difficult for moderates to avoid taking sides. While there are a few important exceptions, overall, sportsmen and environmental groups act as if they have almost nothing to do with each other. Most of the national group leaders have never met and could not even name each other if asked. At times, they act like enemies. Both sides would benefit from being kinder and better listeners, and investing some time to understand each other. More importantly, the conservation cause would benefit.

AMERICAN WILDLIFE CONSERVATION PARTNERS

Members of these organizations represent hunting conservation.

- Archery Trade Association
- Association of Fish and Wildlife Agencies
- Boone and Crockett Club
- Buckmasters American Deer Foundation
- Camp Fire Club of America
- Catch a Dream Foundation
- Congressional Sportsman's Foundation
- Conservation Force
- Dallas Safari Club
- Delta Waterfowl Foundation
- Ducks Unlimited
- Houston Safari Club
- International Hunter Education Association
- Izaak Walton League of America
- Masters of Foxhounds Association of America
- Mule Deer Foundation
- National Assembly of Sportsmen's Caucuses
- National Rifle Association
- National Shooting Sports Foundation
- National Trappers Association
- National Wild Turkey Federation
- North American Bear Foundation
- North American Grouse Partnership
- Orion—The Hunter's Institute
- Pheasants Forever
- Pope and Young Club
- Quail Unlimited
- Quality Deer Management Association
- Rocky Mountain Elk Foundation
- Ruffed Grouse Society
- Safari Club International
- Sand County Foundation
- Shikar Safari Club
- Texas Wildlife Association
- The Wildlife Society
- Theodore Roosevelt Conservation Partnership
- U.S. Sportsmen's Alliance
- Whitetails Unlimited
- Wildlife Forever
- Wildlife Habitat Council
- Wildlife Management Institute

UNDERSTANDING HUNTERS

In 1995, I attended my first Green Group retreat at Robert Redford's Sundance resort. At an evening orientation session, I tried to explain a bit about hunting to nonhunters. It went like this:

If you would, relax and join me for a minute in imagining the verdant North American continent, before Europeans arrived. This is the world of the Labrador duck, sea mink, Carolina parakeet, the swift fox, and the black-footed ferret. Passenger pigeons darken the skies in the Midwest, and roost in such numbers that they break the branches off trees.

Waves of colorful songbirds wash across the entire landscape each spring, filling the air with their elaborate melodies. Bison, pronghorn, elk and mule deer cover the awesome distance of the western plains. Predators, always vigilant for signs of weakness, protect the health of the herd's staggering abundance. A procession of waterfowl species fill the wetlands and waterways for a few weeks each spring and fall.

Great chestnut trees dominate the eastern deciduous forest. Arboreal creatures, such as squirrels, can travel hundreds of miles without touching the ground. Elk live east to Pennsylvania; woodland caribou browse south to Minnesota and Maine. Cougars and wolves live throughout the continent in great climax forests of mature trees, broken by openings made by natural fire.

Clear streams host populations of fish so thick early explorers claimed "that you can almost walk across the water on their backs." Ancient lineages of massive sturgeon inhabit most rivers, with a complex assemblage of freshwater bivalves in the riverbed below them. Grayling are abundant in Michigan, and "blue pike" are common in Lake Erie. Migrations of salmon choke rivers along the northwest and northeast coasts.

Join that world to ours for a moment, and imagine with me that your life is totally dependent on your relationship with this wildlife world. Your interaction with the natural world and its inhabitants is central to your very existence. Your intimate knowledge of this world is at once inherently practical, deeply spiritual—even religious.

Imagine rising well before dawn. In the early morning darkness we walk silently to a chosen place that is revered and sacred. This is a place handed down for generations. It is integral to our self-awareness, and responsible for the survival of our clan for generations. Nearby is a traditional game trail, buffalo wallow, waterhole, salt lick, historic turkey roost, grouse lek, or marsh staging ground for ducks and geese.

To you, the spot is as beautiful as any temple or any human-made place, but even more powerful because it helps give you and those you love life itself. All of your friends and loved ones depend on it for their very existence, for their food.

We cover ourselves completely with clothing made to look like our surroundings, and paint the skin we cannot cover. We may sit for a long time, so we put a piece of our staple, venison jerky, in our mouth and let it sit there. Its taste is as familiar as our own name. In our deep and absolute stillness and silence we become, in effect, almost invisible to the natural world around us.

Oblivious to us, songbirds land on our feet and the tip of our weapon. Squirrels scurry up and down the tree we sit against. The familiar symphony of avians, amphibians and mammals around us is deeply comforting. Our intimate knowledge of these sounds tells us much about those lives.

At times, we attempt to imitate this music. We use several game calls: turkey, cow elk, deer grunt, bull elk, duck, goose, and crow. This makes us even more a part of the natural scene around us, and even more invisible to the creatures around us. Wild animals come by. Eventually, one walks just a few feet upwind. Sometimes, we are able to stalk to within a few body lengths. Often enough, that animal is taken with great skill, care and joy, to become our sustenance, our clothing, and our shelter.

Today, the urgency of this practice is, obviously, long gone. Like many profoundly spiritual or religious pursuits, much of the practice has become lost, perverted, cheapened by technology, or sold out to commercialization.

For some, however, there is a powerful connection that remains. The remnants of the ancient connection with that world and the beauty of it are not yet entirely lost to some of us.

That is why we hunt.

For twenty-five years, I worked for the Izaak Walton League of America, a politically middle-of-the-road conservation organization founded in 1922. Most league members, though not all, are hunters and anglers. The league has an enlightened set of commonsense policies, set by its members, that support everything from international family planning assistance to the right of law-abiding citizens to own and use firearms. We joked that the league was either the greenest hunting group or the most-well-armed environmentalists. The national office in Washington does not set league policy. Its policies come up from small towns and cities across the nation.

On literally hundreds of occasions, I attended chapter meetings in small towns or Midwestern cities where the Pledge of Allegiance was followed by the Member's Pledge: "To Strive for the purity of water, clarity of air, and the wise stewardship of the land and its resources; to know the beauty and understanding of nature and the value of wildlife, woodlands and open space: to the preservation of this heritage and to man's sharing in it. I pledge myself as a member of the Izaak Walton League of America." Often as not, the members would then sit down and describe why they did not like those damned environmentalists.

At one of these meetings near Stevens Point, Wisconsin, a Sierra Club activist attended. She was stunned by the member's knowledge of rare plants and their immediate and overwhelming support for moving an archery target because a rare form of a trailing arbutus plant was found nearby. These were not the stereotypical hunters she had imagined. One of my Green Group colleagues, the head of a successful environmental group, was fond of referring to hunters as "bubbas." As a gay man who had certainly felt the bite of prejudice, he would not have thought of using any of a number of pejoratives to stereotype other groups. I always wondered why this pejorative was somehow okay.

After twenty-five years of working closely with hunters, anglers, and environmentalists, I think the differences between these diverse constituencies are not as great as it sounds from how they treat each other publicly and privately. Both groups believe that habitat protection is paramount for maintaining healthy wildlife populations. There is a great deal of misunderstanding between these groups, arising from a lack of contact and dialogue, and the polarizing effect of the more strident representatives of both groups. Environmentalists complain that hunters seem to rarely assert their political power toward conservation ends, but they can point to very few times when they went to sportsmen for advice and listened to them on strategy or solutions. Some environmentalists are anti-hunting, which is still a minority view in the United States, but goes a long way with sportsmen who fear the impacts of the historic decline in hunting and fishing participation. Other environmentalists identify conservation as a liberal cause or even worse as a wing of the so-called "progressive" movement. This makes it hard for them to find common cause with hunters who own guns and might vote Republican, no matter how ethical, responsible, or committed to conservation they are. According to the human dimensions research group Responsive Management, hunters' political affiliations are Republican, 35 percent; Democrat, 21 percent; and Independent, 28 percent.

Environmentalists complain that hunters are particularly timid about gun issues and the National Rifle Association, even when the NRA promotes a really bad idea like the 2008 rule allowing loaded firearms to be carried in national parks. They call this the poacher protection act, since having readily available firearms will make it easier for illegal poaching of park wildlife where hunting is usually prohibited. They point out how ruthless the NRA has been, even with some of their own. Jim Zumbo is one of the nation's great pro-gun hunters and writers. One day in 2007 he stated the obvious on his blog that he did not think hunters needed assault rifles (fully automatic firearms with large magazine capacity) in order to hunt. Within days, his TV show was suspended, he was dropped as the *Outdoor Life* hunting editor, and several endorsement contracts were cancelled.

In 2005, the Sierra Club sponsored a dinner at the Outdoor Writers Association of America (OWAA) annual conference. Founded in 1927, OWAA was set up to improve the professional skills, set the ethical standards, and help outdoor writers encourage the conservation of natural resources. They invited a hunting icon known as an eloquent and passionate speaker, Newfoundland wildlife biologist and writer Shane Mahoney, to keynote the dinner. Shane gave a great speech, reminding the audience that about 20 percent of Sierra Club members hunt—four times the national average. He implored hunters to work with environmentalists, making the case that the outdoor legacy was too important to let petty differences get in the way. Most OWAA members appreciated the outreach effort by the Sierra Club. The next day at the conference, however, a National Rifle Association representative delivered a harsh condemnation of the Sierra Club from the same podium. Both the Sierra Club and the NRA were OWAA supporting members at the time. The OWAA board supported the NRA's right to disagree with the Sierra Club but objected to the tone of the NRA speech against them. In response, the NRA and about 20 percent of the OWAA members quit the association.

GETTING THE LEAD OUT

A great example of how this lack of understanding between hunters and environmentalists hurts wildlife across the nation is found in efforts to phase out outdated lead bullets and move to using high-tech copper ammunition. Research from state fish and game agencies show that most lead bullets are pulverized on contact with big game. This can contaminate the meat we bring home, as well as the offal piles we leave behind and the scavengers who consume it.

As so often happens, this issue has become unnecessarily polarized. In 2009, the Wildlife Society, the highly respected professional association of the nation's wildlife biologists—and a rare place where hunters, anglers, and environmentalists do talk—called for a measured phase-out of the use of lead bullets. Lead shot for duck hunting was banned in 1991, and the data on contamination of scavengers from bullet fragments now convinced these scientists that a phase-out was justified by the science. Unfortunately, at just about the same time, the radical Center for Biological Diversity petitioned EPA to ban the manufacture of all lead bullets for all purposes. The Wildlife Society did not feel that a ban for all uses was scientifically justified. The action by the environmental groups became a setback for reducing the use of lead in the field. The use of lead for target shooting accounts for 98 percent of its use and presents little exposure to humans or wildlife. What exposure there is can be managed to eliminate what little risk there is. Suddenly, the effort to phase out lead bullets could be painted as anti-shooting of all kinds.

The risk to humans and wildlife from lead bullets is real. In a North Dakota study of 738 blood tests, people who ate a lot of wild game had higher lead levels than those who ate little or none. The more recent the consumption of wild game harvested with lead bullets, the higher the level of lead in the blood. While the amount of lead was below action levels for adults, it was too high for children. The Minnesota and

North Dakota Departments of Health now urge no consumption of any game shot with a lead bullet for pregnant women and children under the age of six. They advised food pantries across the states to not distribute or use donated ground venison because of contamination with lead fragments. According to the North Dakota Department of Agriculture, if these lead fragments had been found in beef, the meat would have been recalled.

A Minnesota Game and Fish study used seventy-two previously euthanized sheep as surrogates for deer. The sheep were shot, skinned, cleaned, and analyzed by radiograph. Researchers found an average of 141 fragments per carcass that dispersed far from the wound channel—an average maximum distance of eleven inches. Fragments were found so far from the exit wound that routine trimming likely would not remove all of the lead. Most lead particles in venison are too small to see, feel, or sense when chewing.

Lead has been known for centuries to be a broad-spectrum toxin for humans and wildlife. In general, the young are at higher risk because they absorb more lead than adults do, and their developing brains are more easily damaged by the lead. Most of the effects are subtle and cannot be easily recognized. The US EPA calls lead "one of the most dangerous neurotoxins in the environment." Lead has been banned in paint, gasoline, toys, plumbing pipes, and even tire balancing weights. In 1991, the US Fish and Wildlife Service ordered a ban on the use of lead shot for hunting migratory waterfowl. About one million ducks, geese, and swans were dying each year from eating spent lead shot pellets.

In Jackson Hole, leading research at Beringia South has found that 50 percent of ravens have elevated blood levels of iron during the hunting season but only 2 percent did during the non-hunting season. Females have significantly higher levels than males. In the pristine Greater Yellowstone ecosystem, 85 percent of the bald eagles tested have elevated lead—more than half at levels that cause impairment. An average of 160 fragments of lead is found in elk gut piles left by hunters, which scavengers then consume.

Hunters contribute a great deal to wildlife conservation—through license fees, an excise tax on gear, the purchase of habitat conservation stamps, and donations to wildlife conservation groups. Given this great record, none of us should want to contaminant our hunt by bringing home tainted meat or leaving toxic lead in the field. We now have good alternatives that allow us to prevent both. In Arizona, 90 percent of hunters in regions critical to the endangered California condor have voluntarily switched to copper. Scientists tell us that without a total ban on lead bullets in the range on the endangered California condor, America's largest bird will cease to exist. If it does, it will be the first time in over a century that hunters have been responsible for the extirpation of a species. While only 6 percent of Americans hunt, 80 percent support legal hunting. By being responsible in the field, hunters can keep it that way.

Most years, I am lucky enough to make a killing shot on an elk using copper bullets. Advanced ballistics make these bullets very accurate. They are more expensive. But it is nice to come home and process the elk with no second thoughts about the lead I brought home or left behind.

HUNTERS, NONHUNTERS, AND NONGAME WILDLIFE

With sportsmen and environmentalists, the misunderstandings go both ways, and both sides have valid points. Most often, environmentalists focus on legal infrastructure and legislative change. Hunters and anglers tend to focus on natural resource budgets and habitat work on the ground. Both areas are important to conservation success. Not surprisingly, hunting leaders want to know why environmentalists will not put their money into conservation action on the ground.

At the beginning of the twentieth century, America's once-numerous game species were largely depleted due to habitat loss and unregulated hunting. In the United States, fish and wildlife are owned by the states, which have jurisdiction over their welfare and management. The federal government shares jurisdiction with the states for migratory species, such as waterfowl. The federal government can assert jurisdiction over species deemed to be "threatened or endangered" with extinction under the Endangered Species Act. The states needed help, especially when it came to the many migratory species that cross state lines.

Each year, Americans spend over $120 billion on hunting, fishing, and wildlife-dependent recreation, according to a survey done by the US Departments of Interior and Commerce. The states and the federal government collect a great deal of sales and income tax on this activity, very little of which finds its way back into the natural resources that support this activity. As with any business, failure to invest in capital infrastructure will eventually lead to a decline. For decades, sportsmen have dealt with this inequity by taxing themselves.

In 1936, during another economically troubled time in our nation's history, sportsmen and wildlife managers persuaded Congress to pass the Pittman-Robertson Act, which established an excise tax on firearms and ammunition dedicated to the conservation of wildlife. In 1950, the Dingell-Johnson Act placed a similar excise tax on sport fishing equipment, and in 1984 the Wallop-Breaux amendment added dedicated fuel taxes attributed to motorboats for conservation purposes. Over the last seventy-five years, excise taxes on hunting and fishing gear have generated over $11 billion dollars in Fish and Wildlife restoration funding for "on the ground" wildlife and habitat protection. In 2009 alone, almost $1 billion was collected and put into wildlife management and habitat work on the ground. Hunting and fishing licenses paid for by sportsmen also generate substantial revenue for state fish and wildlife management. On top of both the federal excise tax and state hunting and fishing licenses, many states also require wildlife habitat conservation stamps. In Wyoming, for example, all hunting and fishing licenses must have a habitat conservation stamp that costs $12.50. A $15 federal duck stamp for waterfowl hunting is required in all states, and many states have their own duck stamp as well. On top of all of this, sportsmen and women voluntarily give millions to groups like Ducks Unlimited, Rocky Mountain Elk Foundation, Pheasants Forever, the Izaak Walton League, Trout Unlimited, and other groups. Sportsmen contribute directly to habitat in all these ways.

Almost all of this revenue is targeted for work on species that are hunted and fished. When game species habitat is protected, however, there are definitely ancillary benefits to nongame species that use the same area, but there is no similar fund that is dedicated for work on these nongame species. Over 85 percent of our wildlife are not game species. Since there are no funds directly targeted to their well-being, nongame species are usually the ones that are most threatened. Without dedicated funding, the research, management, and restoration work does not occur. There have been several attempts by wildlife interests, including sportsmen, to create a similar fund for nongame species. Proposals for excise taxes on binoculars, sleeping bags, backpacks, and other recreational gear have been defeated several times. Imagine what a dedicated fund like this could do to prevent "at risk" wildlife species from becoming endangered or threatened.

In 2004–2005 I was part of a diverse working group asked by a bipartisan group of six US senators to find some common ground to make the Endangered Species Act (ESA) more efficient and effective. Under the auspices of the nonpartisan Keystone Center, we met several times over the course of a year working to craft solutions for Congress to consider. The entire group agreed that funding the act is crucial to species survival and to making the law function better for landowners. But the establishment of an excise tax on backpacks and other outdoor gear for a nongame species fund remains undone. Ironically, this approach has received the most support from hunters, who already contribute a great deal. The visionary and altruistic outdoor equipment outfitter Bass Pro Shops has been a consistent supporter of this kind of approach, but most other major equipment outfitters have not. Ambivalence or even opposition from some environmentalists or the outfitters they patronize has been part of the reason these initiatives have failed. Surprisingly, REI, which calls itself the world's premier outdoor gear store, has been a leading opponent of this approach, as have outdoor outfitters LL Bean and Cabela's.

The 280 million people who visit a national park every year probably care as much for wildlife as sportsmen do but give very little to support wildlife species in comparison to the hunters and anglers. They need a mechanism for participation such as those used by sportsmen and women. Due to chronic funding shortfalls, our parks and their wildlife populations are deteriorating more and more each year. National parks suffer from a $580 million annual operating shortfall and a backlog of maintenance projects that exceeds $9 billion. Basic habitat protection projects in and around parks could use at least that much support. Years of effort to address this budgetary shortfall through the congressional appropriations process have not worked. Park lovers need to take a lesson from sportsmen if they want these national treasures, America's best idea according to filmmaker Ken Burns, to be protected.

With 280 million visits to national parks alone, a $10 heritage and habitat conservation stamp could yield over $1–2 billion per year nationwide. At $10, this fee would cost park visitors less than the federal duck stamp ($15), the typical state habitat conservation stamps paid by sportsmen ($12.50 in Wyoming), or the $50 average paid per Minnesotan for their new conservation sales tax. By including a purchase point explanation at park entrances on why the stamp is needed, this approach would also provide an important educational service that might assist other related conservation efforts. Most Americans do not realize that hunters and anglers invest much more money in the well-being of wildlife than any other sector of our society. There is strong evidence that park visitors and wildlife watchers care just as much and would be willing to pitch in if they were provided a reliable and easy way to do so.

WORKING TOGETHER

Conservation easements are voluntary land protection agreements that have become our most effective and powerful tool for enabling open space and habitat protection on private land. The voluntary legal agreements are simple and extremely flexible. When landowners agree that part or all of their land will never be developed, the reduced value of the land is documented by a qualified appraisal. An easement is then contracted with a qualifying nonprofit organization that will monitor the terms of the agreement "in perpetuity." The Internal Revenue Service treats the diminished value like any other noncash donation to a qualified nonprofit organization. Over thirty-seven million acres has been voluntarily protected in this way—acreage equal to sixteen Yellowstone Parks or the states of Maine, New Hampshire, Vermont, and Massachusetts together. This mechanism is used by sportsmen groups like Ducks Unlimited, Pheasants Forever, and the Rocky Mountain Elk Foundation; by large national conservation groups like the Nature Conservancy, the Conservation Fund, and the Trust for Public Land; and by hundreds of small land trusts nationwide.

In 2005, a shortsighted proposal to do away with tax deductions for voluntary conservation easements was proposed and gaining momentum in the US Congress. In 2006, with the help of the Association of Fish and Wildlife Agencies that represents state fish and wildlife agencies in Washington, these groups sent a letter to Congress to support the tax deduction for these voluntary land protection agreements. When elected officials saw such widespread bipartisan support for conservation easements, momentum shifted dramatically on Capitol Hill. The shortsighted proposal to eliminate tax deductions for conservation easements was defeated.

Ironically, when environmentalists offered to sign the letter as well, some sportsmen groups balked at being on the same letter with the green groups. I took the exact same letter, found twenty environmental groups eager to sign it, and sent it to Congress separately. When the legislation was enacted, not only were the conservation tax deductions retained, they were strengthened and improved with more safeguards against abuse. Congress even provided more generous terms for donors of voluntary conservation easements on private land by extending the number of years over which the tax deductions could be spread and increasing the total deduction allowed. When hunters and land conservationists used their power for conservation together, the results were dramatic.

Though more uncommon, when sportsmen and environmentalists do work together, the results are equally impressive. The Wildlife Management Institute is a policy think tank founded in 1911. In 1995, the executive director, Rollin Sparrowe, brought together a remarkable diversity of groups in support of national wildlife refuges. Called the Cooperative Alliance for Refuge Enhancement, it has been a rare example of what sportsmen and environmentalists can do when they work together. The group is extremely diverse, with the National Rifle Association and Safari Club International working with Defenders of Wildlife and the National Audubon Society. Whenever diverse groups like this visit a member of Congress, they get attention. Almost as large as the national park system, national wildlife refuges total over 150 million acres, one and a half times the size of the state of California. Historically, wildlife refuges have received only a fraction of the funding per acre as national parks. The groups came together to address the operations and maintenance backlog on our 550 national wildlife refuges. Today, that backlog remains at $3.7 billion, but the groups have succeeded in keeping that decline from becoming worse. At a time when all natural resource funding has been severely cut, national wildlife refuges have seen an increase of $100 million. Even with this unprecedented increase, in fiscal year 2010, the National Wildlife Refuge System received $3.25 per acre in federal appropriations while the National Park Service received $32 per acre.

NATURAL ALLIES

The Cooperative Alliance for Refuge Enhancement (CARE) is a coalition of conservation, recreation, sporting, and scientific organizations that has been working in common cause since 1995 to promote funding for the National Wildlife Refuge System.

- American Birding Association
- American Fisheries Society
- American Sportfishing Association
- Association of Fish and Wildlife Agencies
- Congressional Sportsmen's Foundation
- Defenders of Wildlife
- Ducks Unlimited
- Izaak Walton League of America
- Marine Conservation Biology Institute
- National Audubon Society
- National Rifle Association of America

- National Wildlife Federation
- National Wildlife Refuge Association
- Safari Club International
- The Corps Network
- The Wilderness Society
- The Wildlife Society
- Trout Unlimited
- U.S. Sportsmen's Alliance
- Wildlife Forever
- Wildlife Management Institute

Sportsmen continue to be a leading voice on other key environmental issues like wetland protection, farm conservation, climate change, and responsible energy development. They were key to stopping some ill-advised proposed sales of public lands. They are leaders in combating wildlife diseases, such as chronic wasting disease. Sportsmen's groups have become increasingly active on climate change and the widespread impact it will have on wildlife habitats that have taken so many years and so much effort to protect. In all these cases, and many others, sportsmen figured out these issues on their own, only to hear some environmentalists erroneously take credit for "getting sportsmen involved."

This dynamic can change. In 2011, the largest coalition ever of recreation, hunting, angling, and environmental groups came together over their shared interest in conservation funding. With twelve hundred organization members, America's Voice for Conservation, Recreation, and Preservation holds the potential for being a powerful voice and a breakthrough constituency group.

RURAL RESIDENTS

Theodore Roosevelt IV is the great grandson of Pres. Theodore Roosevelt. He has served on the boards of several major national conservation and environmental groups: the Pew Center for Climate Change, World Resources Institute, the Wilderness Society, and Trout Unlimited. Ted and I served together on the national board of the League of Conservation Voters. A few years ago Ted wrote that many rural Americans feel that environmentalists do not understand or are not sympathetic to them. They feel that environmentalists are dismissive and condescending. Even worse, many rural Americans feel the environmentalists demonize them.

Yet both groups have much in common. Whether they choose to live in rural areas or visit whenever they can, both groups love the outdoors, nature, and the undeveloped landscape. Throughout much of this landscape, private landowners are key to species preservation. At least 60 percent of threatened species are found on private land, with 90 percent spending some portion of their life cycle on private land. There is no doubt that most rural Americans love the land as much as anyone, a concept that polling results support. There is every reason to believe rural America wants a healthy natural environment, even if they sometimes elect people who do not always vote that way.

For rural residents from small towns used to closing business deals with a handshake, some environmentalist's tactics cause mistrust. We see this in northwest Wyoming where a compromise has limited snowmobile access in the iconic Yellowstone Park to roads only, using cleaner four-stroke machines, accompanied by a licensed guide, and with a daily limit on the total number of machines allowed to enter the park. Most people agree that requiring cleaner machines, putting a cap on the number of machines allowed per day, and prohibiting off road use is essential in Yellowstone Park. It has, however, been hard for rural families who have been going into the park for years on their own, and who have never done anything wrong, to understand why they now have to hire an expensive guide to do so. Still, despite this compromise that has solved most of the problems that unrestrained snow machine use once caused, many environmentalists continue to fight for a total ban on snowmobiles on park roads. They are seemingly oblivious to the political cost of their campaign to progress on much higher-priority wildlife habitat issues that require the support of rural people in the Greater Yellowstone region. Many of these rural residents see the Yellowstone snowmobile fight as more of a cultural than environmental issue. Telling each other how to recreate has never been a good way to build bridges.

Yellowstone wildlife cannot survive the critical winter season without access to private land owned by many of these same rural residents. While the heart of the Greater Yellowstone area is protected in 2.5 million acres of Yellowstone and Grand Teton National Parks, the winter habitat surrounding the park—the habitat most critical to the survival of much of the ecosystem's wildlife—is under-protected and is disappearing rapidly. The region's iconic assemblage of wildlife cannot survive without it, and it cannot be protected without the voluntary cooperation of ranchers and other local people who own the land needed by wildlife to survive the winter. Wildlife scientists identify the 28 million acres as the Greater Yellowstone region. This ecosystem includes:

- An irreplaceable collection of habitats that supports an intact collection of wildlife species not found anywhere else, including all the species that have lived here since Europeans arrived;
- The location of the five remaining longest long-distance mammal migrations—one of the earth's most stunning and imperiled biological phenomena—in the lower forty-eight states;
- Habitat for large concentrations of elk, mule deer, mountain sheep, bison, and pronghorn, and the southern anchor of a larger

system for wide-ranging carnivores that are critical to the natural balance: wolves, bears, mountain lions, wolverine, lynx, coyotes, and fox;

- Home to 109 other species or communities considered to be imperiled globally, including critical habitat for the world's largest swan, the trumpeter swan;

- *Thermus aquaticus*, the heat-loving bacteria that were used to isolate enzymes that allowed the DNA identification that has allowed so many crimes to be solved.

This remarkable region inspires as much passion and conservation altruism as any other place on earth. Early explorers to the region, during the heyday era of "manifest destiny," gave up their right to make significant claims of private ownership. In 1872, they convinced Congress to establish the area as a national park "held to the unrestricted use of the people." Subsequent generations put five times the park acreage into national forests that surround Yellowstone Park. They put a halt to poaching and illegal logging and convinced Congress to establish Grand Teton National Park.

At the current rate of permanent habitat loss, the extraordinary wildlife that characterizes the Greater Yellowstone region will not be maintained for future generations. A primary focus on voluntary habitat protection agreements primarily with ranchers and other private landowners can ensure that future generations will experience Yellowstone much as we have. Is this really the place where we want to alienate local residents in order to get the last few snow machines off the roads in Yellowstone Park during the dead of winter? Ironically, no one is advocating closing the one road in Yellowstone Park that is kept open to cars in winter, even though that is the only area where wildlife are found all year long.

Ted Roosevelt summarized the situation this way: "It is time for the environmental community to take a hard, critical look at ourselves with regard to our treatment of rural people and our resultant standing in those communities. This is important, not just from a political perspective, but from an ecological and humanistic one. If we continue our business-as-usual approach or pursue inauthentic remedies, we will continue to alienate a large, vulnerable and critical sector of the American electorate."

One summer, I spent a few days at a ranch owned by an environmental leader who allowed that he would love to have a pronghorn antelope mount for his ranch. They were so beautiful, but he feared that some of his supporters would not understand. The next day I was at a meeting of hunting leaders at the Safari Club International's wilderness training center. The hunting groups started off each meal with an environmental saying or nature poem. In their library was a portrait of the environmental heroine Margaret Murie. The actual differences between hunters and environmentalists have always reminded me of Mark Twain's comment after hearing his first opera: "It is not as bad as it sounds." When they come together for conservation, they are unstoppable.

9

The Minnesota Miracles

Real Success through Engagement

Some luck lies in not getting what you thought you wanted
but getting what you have, which once you have got it you may be
smart enough to see is what you would have wanted had you known.
—Minnesota native Garrison Keillor

A thing is right when it tends to preserve the integrity, stability,
and beauty of the biotic community. It is wrong when it tends otherwise.
—Aldo Leopold

A N EXTRAORDINARY EXAMPLE of the breakthrough progress that is possible when environmentalists, sportsmen, and rural residents work together comes from my home state of Minnesota. In 2008, after a ten-year grassroots citizen effort to gain the right to vote on it, Minnesotan citizens got a conservation funding measure on the ballot in 2008. They did it above the objections of many of their elected leaders and of most of the state's editorial media. The initiative called for a 3/8 percent sales tax dedicated to conservation. Once they were able to place the compromise initiative on the ballot, it passed by a margin of 57–39 percent, even though not voting counted against the measure as a "no" vote. It received the most votes of any candidate or issue in Minnesota history. It did so as a taxing and spending initiative during the worse economic recession in seventy-five years.

The Minnesota initiative yields over $270 million per year for clean water, wildlife habitat protection, cultural restoration, and land conservation—about $7.5 billion over the twenty-five-year life of the program. The initiative will cost the average Minnesotan about four cents on a $10 purchase, or about $50 per adult per year. It is enough money to assure the stewardship of a significant representation of the Minnesota landscape—forever. With the leverage and incentives for other funding that this much new money provides, it will be enough to enable "the land of ten thousand lakes" to secure a sustainable landscape for the future. It passed despite opposition from the state's Governor Tim Pawlenty and 95 percent of the state's media, many of whom philosophically oppose ballot initiatives. Success required a diverse leadership, from groups that often did not work together, who stuck together through years of adversity.

One key to success was the unlikely state senator Bob Lessard. Lessard is a classic northern Minnesota iron-range conservative who has fought with environmentalists for years. Like 1.5 million other people in Minnesota, which has the highest percentage of people who hunt and fish of any state in the United States, Bob likes to catch and shoot. As a state legislator, he knew first hand that adequate funding for wildlife would never come from the state capitol; it needed to come from the people. In the early 1990s, he was part of a successful effort by Minnesota duck hunters to raise $750,000 to buy the US Fish and Wildlife Service an enforcement helicopter to stop the poaching epidemic in Louisiana. On the heels of that successful effort, he proposed a dedicated 1/8 percent addition to the state sales tax dedicated to wildlife conservation and management, modeled on the one passed in Missouri in 1984. His proposal went nowhere.

In late 2004 and early 2005 a series of articles in the *Minneapolis Star Tribune* documented the decline in Minnesota hunting, fishing, and water quality. A full 40 percent of the famous ten thousand lakes are not safe for fishing and swimming according to federal clean water standards. The state has already lost at least 50 percent of its original wetlands and 90 percent of its prairie wetlands. Less than 4 percent of its original old-growth forests remained. If it were to survive, Minnesota's cherished outdoor heritage needed a dedicated new source of funding. Suddenly, duck hunters and bird watchers realized that they needed each other and were talking to each other. They started the "Vote Yes for Water Quality" campaign to pass this ballot initiative.

This is the wording of the actual ballot initiative:

<u>Clean Water, Wildlife, Cultural Heritage and Natural Areas:</u>
"Shall the Minnesota Constitution be amended to dedicate funding to protect our drinking water sources; to protect, enhance, and restore our wetlands, prairies, forests, and fish, game, and wildlife habitat; to preserve our arts and cultural heritage; to support our parks and trails; and to protect, enhance, and restore our lakes, rivers, streams, and groundwater by increasing the sales and use tax rate beginning July 1, 2009, by three-eighths of one percent on taxable sales until the year 2034."

On Earth Day 2005, the struggle to get the initiative on the ballot, where Minnesotans could vote it up or down, began in earnest. Over seven thousand people from the left, right, and center of Minnesota politics gathered in front of the state capital in St. Paul, united by their love of the outdoors. I was on the speaker's stage, as the leader of one of the supporting organizations. Notable among the speakers was Bud Grant, the legendary and beloved former coach of the Minnesota Vikings—who took the team to the Super Bowl four times but never won. This time, he and the state of Minnesota would win a victory far better than the Super Bowl. The groups had formed the Coalition for Ducks, Wetlands, and Clean Water. What had always been a disparate crowd was becoming a solid working alliance.

The rally was within sight of the governor's office, on the front lawn of the state legislature. This diverse group of citizens required the attention of the political leaders—many of whom feared the loss of control this dedicated fund initiative represented. By operating openly and with respect for their groups' differences, the coalition stuck together for over three years—building the support they needed to convince a reluctant state legislature to allow their initiative to be put on the ballot in 2008. Looking back, the diverse leaders of the coalition credit their success with what is called "Minnesota nice"—the traditional behavior of long-time Minnesota residents to be courteous, reserved, and mild mannered. Garrison Keillor famously describes it as "where all the women are strong, all the men are good-looking, and all the children are above average." They also credited some extraordinarily dedicated volunteer leadership that typified that attitude.

Dave Zentner is a retired Duluth businessman known for his outdoor skills as a fly fisherman and bird hunter, as well as his conservation ethic and diplomatic ability. He was one of the volunteer citizen leaders who gave hundreds of days and thousands of miles on the road to the effort over several years. Zentner is the prototypical hunter-angler conservationist—green, pragmatic, and persistent. He has won several national conservation awards and an honorary doctorate from the University of Minnesota–Duluth for his lifetime of effort and accomplishment at bringing people together. He loves Minnesota and loves the outdoors. During a long career as a financial planner and insurance consultant, his dedication to conservation had cost him business and income—both from time out of the office and from people who would not do business with him due to his public leadership on some issues. Dave is the quintessential example of Minnesota nice. "We always knew that if green and guns ever came together in the cause of wildlife conservation, they would be unstoppable," said Zentner. "In Minnesota, we proved that with 'Vote Yes for Water Quality and Wildlife' initiative."

Minnesota has other examples of durable success from people working together and failures when they have not. In the late 1980s there were several examples of both.

In the early 1970s Minnesota's major utility, Northern States Power, decided to build two enormous nuclear energy plants. They did so along the Mississippi River on land belonging to the Mdewakanton Sioux Indian people. The land was open, next to the continent's most reliable water supply, the landowners were willing, and Indian ownership of the land helped them avoid some regulatory issues. At the time, the federal government had promised to take ownership of the nuclear waste. To this day, that is a promise they have never been able to fulfill. When the federal government considered options for a permanent national nuclear waste repository, northern Minnesota's stable multibillion-year-old Precambrian bedrock was on the short list of best sites from a purely geological perspective. Not wanting nuclear waste storage in their backyard, the Minnesota legislature quickly passed a bill prohibiting any permanent storage of nuclear waste in the state of Minnesota—even though the state depended heavily on its three nuclear power plants.

In 1987 Congress made a political decision to put the facility in a much less geologically stable formation within Yucca Mountain in Nevada and promised again that it would begin accepting waste from the nation's 104 nuclear power plants for permanent storage in 1998. Nevada is a state with no nuclear plants of its own, where citizens have expressed heavy opposition to having the nation's nuclear waste repository imposed on them. After over thirty years of work, and ten billion dollars in costs, in 2009 Energy Secretary Steven Chu finally conceded that this site was not geologically suitable and was "off the table." Even if this site had been certified, it would not have been able to accept all the waste that today's existing nuclear plants would produce. Another site would be needed. Now, no one knows where America's nuclear waste will end up.

In 1990, Congress's promise to begin to accept nuclear waste by 1998 did not solve Minnesota's problem. Their nuclear plants were already out of storage capacity. Northern States Power company pro-

posed dry cask "temporary" storage on site. There were several problems with this idea: the high cost of building on-site storage, the fact
that the site was on a flood plain that had been inundated in a 1963
flood, the Indian landowners did not want it, and the Minnesota state
government had banned nuclear waste storage in the state.

I was working on an evaluation of alternatives and was called as a
witness during the contested case hearing before the Minnesota Public
Utility Board. In the debate that ensued, we established the fact that
the Westinghouse steam generators in the nuclear plant were of the
same type found to be defective in the Oregon's Trojan nuclear plant.
Trojan was closed in 1992 after several leaks of radioactive steam from
the defective generators. During Minnesota's contested case hearings
on the issue, Northern States Power denied under oath that there were
any problems with the steam generators. In fact, at the time they were
already secretly negotiating a settlement with Westinghouse—a fact
not made public until years later, after the issue was decided. If the
generator tubes were defective, then the long-term cost-effectiveness
of Minnesota's nuclear power plants needed to be reevaluated.

The Minnesota legislature was deeply and evenly divided on the
issue. The decision on whether to phase out the plant was held by just
a few undecided swing votes. Would storage of nuclear waste on this
site be temporary or permanent, thereby against Minnesota law passed
just a few years earlier to prohibit nuclear waste storage in their state?
They were aware of the fact that nuclear plants are exempt from normal liability. All property owners' insurance policies provide an ex-
emption from coverage in the event of a nuclear accident under the
Price Anderson Act. What was the most likely future cost of nuclear
power? Were the future costs of nuclear energy worth it? If the nation's insurance underwriters would not cover nuclear liability, should
the state take the risk of letting the plants operate? Not only had the
insurance industry refused to insure nuclear plants, investors nationwide had abandoned nuclear energy due to cost overruns and lingering

safety concerns. At that time, in 1990, no new plant had been contracted for over fifteen years, since 1975, and which is still true in 2012. Minnesota was close to phasing out nuclear energy in the state . . . until Greenpeace got involved.

On the evening of a key hearing before the entire state legislature that was televised across the entire state, disruptive protestors had to be removed from the proceeding. Greenpeace activists hung protest messages off billboards in town, and someone dressed in a devil suit chased a key Democratic legislator around the capitol for "making a deal with the devil." Overnight, the issue became identified with extremists and was lost. Regardless of how they viewed the merits of the issue, swing votes in the state legislature were unable or unwilling to be identified with this behavior back in their home districts, especially when it came time for re-election. Today, Minnesota stores nuclear waste in dry casks, essentially big stainless steel thermos bottles, with no end in sight. No one knows where this waste will end up and what the full long-term cost of storing it will be to future generations.

Around the same time, cooperative efforts led to a positive outcome on another major power plant proposal, and two other important conservation issues. I was the Midwest director of the Izaak Walton League at the time and involved in all of these efforts.

PUMPED STORAGE POWER AT LAKE PEPIN

The Southern Minnesota Municipal Power Agency (SMMPA) generated electric power for about ten Minnesota communities. As a municipal power agency, it had fewer regulations than the large public utilities. In 1990 SMMPA proposed a large pumped storage power plant on the hills above Lake Pepin, a natural widening in the Mississippi River about fifty miles downriver from the Twin Cities. They wanted to build a lake at the top of the hill, use low-cost power at night to pump millions of gallons of Lake Pepin water to the top of the hill, then use it during times of peak power need to generate electricity as the water flowed back down the hill. The power loss from the project would be enormous. It would generate far more peak time power than this small utility could use and would use three times that much off-peak power to pump all that water up the hill. This small municipal power group was speculating on the market, using their position as a municipal utility as cover.

The most threatening aspect of the project for the environment was from toxic pollutants stored in the lakebed. Lake Pepin had been the repository of toxins washing down from the Twin Cities for over a century. Most of these toxins had settled in the bottom of the lake where they were relatively stable. Moving this much water out of and back into the lake every day would stir up the sediments—putting them back into the water column and reintroducing the toxins into the lake and the food chain for fish and wildlife. Alternatives were available for lowering peak time power demand much more cost-effectively, without damage to the environment. The project was a very bad idea, but it had some serious and well-connected supporters.

In response, a small group of local citizens started gathering in the office of a nearby commercial orchard every Tuesday evening. I was the only full-time conservationist in the group, invited because of my unique combination of work on both energy policy and Upper Mississippi River habitat issues. We divided up the research tasks, marshaled our facts, and made our case politely to the SMMPA board, which was made up of local leaders. No one hung off billboards, disrupted meetings, or chased elected officials in costumes. Within a few months, the project was cancelled.

DOUBLE HULLS FOR HAZARDOUS CARGO

After the 1988 spill of the Exxon *Valdez*, several natural resource and conservation leaders pointed out that large amounts of petroleum products and other industrial chemical are shipped on barges through five hundred miles of the Mark Twain and Upper Mississippi Wildlife and Fish Refuges between St. Louis and St. Paul. The sinuous channel is laced with submerged rock wing dams, and stranded barges are not uncommon. Twenty-six locks need to be negotiated, often requiring that the barge tow be split in half for lockage. The complex backwaters of these wildlife refuges are heavily used by millions of Mississippi Flyway ducks, geese, and swans. During the long days of the northern spring and summer, these backwaters are among the most biologically productive habitats on earth.

After we raised the issue in the press, a Wisconsin game warden stepped forward to validate our concerns. He knew from firsthand experience the risk at hand. With a heavy river current between five and ten miles per hour on many reaches of the river, a spill would travel twenty-five to fifty miles in the first few hours—contaminating thousands of acres of wetlands before any containment was possible. Very little spill response capacity existed, with none in many reaches of the river. If the spill occurred during the spring or fall migration, millions of birds would perish. It would be far worse than a spill in the open ocean. Many of the better companies had already switched to double hull barges, but 20 percent of the companies had not—giving them a perverse cost advantage over those who did the right thing on their own.

We needed to find a way to get all the hazardous cargo transported in double hulls. Interstate commerce rules did not allow a state to require double hull barges, but the states could require guide boats at the head of each barge carrying hazardous cargo in single hulls. The state of Wisconsin, with bipartisan leadership, quickly enacted this new law. It became more convenient and less costly for the barge companies who were not using double hulls to switch over to double hulls rather than have to use guide boats at the head of the tow. Today, all hazardous cargo carried on barges on the Upper Mississippi is carried in double hulls.

BOUNDARY WATERS CANOE AREA AND
MILITARY OVERFLIGHTS

This example may be the most win-win. Minnesota's most beloved and iconic landscape is the one-million-acre Boundary Waters Canoe Area Wilderness (BWCAW). Thousands of lakes and rivers are separated by relatively short portage trails. Each year tens of thousands of Americans come to enjoy the scenery, wildlife, fishing, and tranquility. Many of us still drink water right out of the middle of a lake. It is a place where the sound of silence is profound. Motors are not allowed on boats, and chain saws and power tools of all kinds are illegal. Based on a 1948 presidential order, aircraft of all kinds must not fly below four thousand feet mean sea level. There may be no other place on earth where so much attention has been given to the auditory aspects of wilderness.

In the 1980s, the Boundary Waters Canoe Area's airspace above four thousand feet became a heavily used Military Operations Area for jet fighters from the Duluth-based National Guard. One evening of a multiday canoe trip, I was walleye fishing on Bald Eagle Lake, about twenty-five miles from the nearest road. A moose was quietly feeding nearby, and there was a military jet dogfight going on about a half-mile overhead (our lake was at about fifteen hundred feet elevation).

We were not alone in our dismay at the disruption of the boundary waters tranquility. In 1987, about one-third of BWCAW visitors reported to the US Forest Service that their trips were disrupted by military training exercises. This included visitors with significant military experience and backgrounds. After exchanging some salvos with the National Guard in the press, conservation groups filed a lawsuit. In my role of Midwest director of the Izaak Walton League, I was one of the co-plaintiffs and a witness at the first hearing to describe my personal experience.

During that year's annual dinner of the Friends of the Boundary

Waters Wilderness, who were leading the action, the issue came up at my table. I made a rookie mistake by not knowing who everyone was before I spouted off: "I don't know why that damn National Guard will not consider a compromise to move their Military Operations Area to the east, in parts of the national forest not over the boundary waters and over Lake Superior. We could preserve the boundary waters and their need for a training area." The guy next to me then introduced himself: "Paul, I am Col. Don Sowald from the National Guard. We need to have lunch." Don, to his credit, had come into the lion's den that evening. At lunch a few days later, I brought a sketch of my alternative. It took us a few months to convince the hard heads in both our camps, but our compromise has now been in place since 1990. The National Guard has its readiness training area and the Boundary Waters Canoe Area Wilderness has its tranquility.

While it provides some of the best examples of the power of compromise and engagement, Minnesota is not unique. Across the nation, the cooperative spirit that led to all these success stories characterizes a big part of the greatest success in conservation of the past thirty years—the local land trusts who are having enormous success protecting the best open space, scenery, and wildlife habitat in their communities.

10
Land Conservation

Example isn't the main thing in influencing others—it is the only thing.
—Albert Schweitzer

Impatience is indispensable to getting reform started;
patience is essential to seeing its promise fulfilled.
—E. J. Dionne

THE STUNNING SUCCESS of the nation's land trusts' efforts at open space conservation, over the same period of time that environmental progress has ground to a halt, is a great example of the power of engagement and a positive "first steps" approach to conservation. If you look at the campaign materials for these land conservation initiatives, you see little strident rhetoric and a lot of practical solutions.

Land trusts are land conservation organizations that include small groups working in local communities and some of the largest conservation organizations working nationally and internationally, such as the Nature Conservancy, the Conservation Fund, the Trust for Public Land, and Conservation International. In 1980, there were only a few land trusts in existence. Today, there are about seventeen hundred land trusts that work locally, but they are organized nationally by the Land

Acres Conserved	2000	2005	2010
Owned by state and local land trusts	1,123,689	1,527,656	2,144,709
Under easement by state and local land trusts	2,316,064	6,007,906	8,833,368
Acquired and reconveyed or conserved by other means by state and local land trusts	2,031,062	3,3707722	5,097,783
Total conserved by state and local land trusts	5,470,815	10,906,334	16,075,860
Total conserved by national land trusts	18,388,023	25,964,032	30,945,639
Total conserved by all land trusts	23,858,838	36,870,366	47,021,499

The success of land trusts in conserving open space is evidence of the appeal of a collaborative approach to conservation. Source: Land Trust Alliance (www.landtrustalliance.org)

Trust Alliance. By 2010, almost fifty million acres had been privately and voluntarily protected by landowners and these groups. This is an area equal to the states of Pennsylvania, Maryland, New Jersey, Delaware, and Connecticut together.

The Nature Conservancy may provide the best single example of the widespread appeal of a collaborative approach to conservation. Founded in 1950, today the Nature Conservancy is the largest conservation group on earth with chapters in all fifty states and programs in thirty-five countries. Their annual budget is almost one billion dollars with assets over four billion dollars. They have protected 119 million acres worldwide—an area almost the size of all the original thirteen US colonies.

The most impressive success of the land trusts is their land conservation ballot initiatives. According to LandVote, a project of the Trust for Public Land, from 1988 to 2012, a time when opposition to taxes became gospel for some, voters approved $57.5 billion in tax increases for open-space bonds and other land conservation initiatives to support the land trusts' efforts. When offered practical solutions and given the chance, Americans vote for conservation solutions—even if it means a tax increase.

SUMMARY OF LAND PROTECTION BALLOT MEASURES
BY YEAR, 1988–PRESENT

Date	Number of Measures	Pass? (tot)	Total Funds Approved (tot)	Conservation Funds Approved (tot)
1988	26	24	$1,951,633,862	$1,422,578,862
1989	29	22	$1,409,488,521	$937,676,870
1990	42	25	$2,376,796,066	$2,292,828,066
1991	16	10	$187,802,360	$168,157,360
1992	36	26	$2,038,626,000	$1,744,941,000
1993	23	19	$600,869,860	$555,665,753
1994	51	33	$1,044,541,125	$621,248,511
1995	41	33	$1,339,112,844	$1,114,619,344
1996	99	71	$5,371,324,178	$1,460,316,498
1997	83	69	$2,600,753,306	$778,514,321
1998	175	143	$7,224,354,744	$5,742,872,774
1999	110	98	$2,426,825,522	$2,099,759,028
2000	207	168	$11,230,270,431	$4,983,222,298
2001	198	138	$1,802,683,640	$1,367,556,655
2002	184	136	$8,573,159,162	$5,486,074,357
2003	126	95	$1,771,740,328	$1,252,196,985
2004	215	161	$26,032,263,413	$3,923,245,265
2005	141	111	$2,618,811,630	$1,598,003,889
2006	183	136	$29,082,431,422	$6,707,041,755
2007	100	66	$2,245,755,926	$1,952,415,707
2008	128	91	$11,102,012,360	$8,046,960,160
2009	40	25	$1,059,164,056	$607,668,083
2010	49	41	$2,378,635,217	$2,186,464,866
2011	24	14	$539,231,467	$312,765,748
2012	11	6	$188,327,900	$31,027,900
TOTALS	**2337**	**1761**	**$127,196,615,340**	**$57,393,822,055**

Every year, citizens vote in favor of bonds and other initiatives to fund land preservation and other conservation measures across the country. *Source: Trust for Public Land, LandVote® Database (www.tpl.org)*

Polling shows that land conservation initiatives are popular everywhere, even in states where local politics prevent citizens from having the right to vote on them. In Idaho, for example, a state with particularly strong anti-tax politicians, polls show strong support and willingness to pay twenty dollars per year to dedicate funds for land conservation. When presented thoughtfully, conservation has overwhelming and widespread appeal. Many other deserving issues have not enjoyed this level of revenue-generating commitment.

The success of land conservation provides a striking contrast to the gridlock of the last twenty years on environmental issues and the recent decline in the environmental issue's popularity. Ironically, the land trust groups could have done even better if they had not had interference from some environmental groups. In 2000, the land trusts and sportsmen groups put together the nation's largest initiative for breakthrough national funding—over one billion dollars per year that would have protected more of America's landscape than anything that had been done since Theodore Roosevelt's time.

The Conservation and Reinvestment Act (CARA) of 1999 presented a remarkable opportunity to advance natural resource conservation, land protection, wildlife habitat restoration, and voluntary open space preservation. It had broad support and was one of the most creative and unusual compromise bills seen in the nation's capital in a long time. For fewer than five dollars per adult American per year, it would have transformed the American landscape by giving people the financial incentives to voluntarily protect a great part of our natural heritage. The bill had strong support of a huge coalition of sixteen hundred state and local recreation and land protection groups, sportsmen and women. The people most knowledgeable and engaged in our nation's wildlife conservation—the professional fish, wildlife, park, and refuge managers and their professional association, such as the Wildlife Society—were among its strongest supporters. Ironically, this visionary initiative was killed by an opposition from some environmentalists who feared that some of the funding might be used for coastal infrastructure, right-wing legislators opposed to land conservation, and jealous members of the appropriations committees in Congress who feared a loss of their pork barrel power.

The lead co-sponsors and key architects of the bill were Rep. George Miller of California, one of the greenest members of Congress, and House Resources Chairman Don Young, one of the least green who once said that he "didn't see any justification for the federal government owning land, other than the Statue of Liberty and maybe a few parks, maybe a few refuges." In the best US tradition, these lawmakers negotiated a historic, albeit not perfect, compromise bill. The bill had 315 co-sponsors, including a majority of both Republicans and Democrats—something not seen in Washington, DC, very often. Unfortunately, in the nation's capital a few obstructionists can stop almost anything.

In an era of declining opportunities for wildlife habitat protection, hunting, fishing, and similar pursuits, CARA would have provided permanent funding for land acquisition, wildlife management, and other key conservation activities, including:

- $1 billion for impact assistance and coastal conservation for thirty-five coastal states and territories;
- $900 million for the Land and Water Conservation Fund, which supplies funding for federal land acquisition and matching grants to states for parks, open space, and other conservation needs;
- $350 million for wildlife conservation and restoration through expansion of the successful federal aid programs;
- $125 million to the Urban Park and Recreation Recovery program;
- $100 million to the Historic Preservation Fund;
- $200 million toward federal and American Indian lands restoration;
- $150 million for permanent conservation easements; and
- $50 million for threatened and endangered species recovery.

It is said that there is nothing new under the sun, and this bill was an example of that. It was a direct outgrowth of efforts started in the late 1950s that directed that part of the royalties for extraction of offshore oil, a nonrenewable resource, should be put into a fund for the support of renewable resources, such as parks and forests. After years of effort Congress agreed, and the Land and Water Conservation Fund (LWCF) was born in 1965.

The LWCF is the most important federal program you have never heard of. Most everyone has spent time in a park or on a ball field that was established by this program. Unfortunately, the people that wrote this legislation did not require that a sign be posted recognizing the source of the funding that made the park possible. The fund was highly successful at first, until lawmakers discovered a loophole and broke the faith with Americans by using the money authorized for conservation in this law for other things. When Congress passed the Land and Water Conservation Fund, it did not make the appropriation of funds permanent and mandatory. In the days before big deficits, who would have thought Congress would use the money to subsidize its free-spending ways in other areas? It was a raw deal for all conservation-minded Americans—environmentalists, hunters, anglers, and outdoor enthusiasts.

Even though the authorized amount of funds is about nine hundred million dollars a year, for the past twenty years Congress has only appropriated that amount once. In most years lawmakers have appropriated less than two hundred million dollars. By 2009, more than fifteen billion dollars from this fund was diverted to other spending. CARA would have righted this wrong while providing assistance to coastal communities to help them cope with the impacts of offshore oil development. When oil is drilled on land, the state gets 50 percent of the royalties; when oil is drilled more than three miles offshore, the state gets nothing. This bill's framers worked diligently to ensure that it would in no way provide an incentive for more offshore oil drilling, a major concern for environmentalists. Decisions on offshore oil projects would be made independently, as they had been for years.

In the US House of Representatives, a majority of both Republicans and Democrats voted in favor of the bill—a rarity then and now. The majorities came from the center, with the far right and far left opposing it. In the US Senate, the obstructionists prevailed. The legislation never came to a vote and the bill died at the end of that Congress.

When given the chance, strong majorities of Americans vote with their wallets for land protection—using whatever mechanism seems most appropriate to local circumstances. In Maryland, when we bought our house in 1996 we paid a 1 percent "real-estate transfer tax" that provided funding for land conservation. In this way, housing demand helps pay for new conservation—a win-win scenario. In Wyoming, where we are allegedly rugged individuals dedicated to local control, the state government prohibits its counties from even considering a real estate transfer levy of any kind—no matter what local people think. Why local decisions on land conservation funding are any of the state's business has not been explained. Some of the real estate industry, not content to merely have this prohibition be a law, are pushing for it to be a constitutional amendment. Still, even Wyoming is building a two-hundred-million-dollar wildlife trust fund. It is much less than what is needed, but it is a start.

Americans love their land. During a time when people have lost faith that their tax dollars are used well, and even during the worst recession in seventy-five years, they are fighting their own elected officials for the right to vote to tax themselves to enable land protection efforts. They are still waiting for their leaders to do their part, by getting behind their constituents who want to see "America the Beautiful" stay that way. The zenith of their success shows the power of respectful engagement and compromise in conservation and provides a stark contrast to the nadir of in-your-face environmentalism.

11

Eating Their Own Young

The Nader Nadir

In some ways, it is easier to be a dissident, for then one is without responsibility.
—Nelson Mandela

Strong and bitter words indicate a weak cause.
—Steve's fortune cookie

R EGARDLESS OF HOW YOU VIEW THE MOTIVATION, in outcome most radical environmentalism is effectively anti-environmental. It drives people away from an issue that is inherently in their best interests and that they are predisposed to support. People are yearning for a way to get their heads around conservation and ecology but don't want to dress up in fish suits, wear funny hats, or be associated with people who come across as strident or unkind. Self-righteousness is not an attractive trait, no matter how vital the cause. Nothing dissuades engagement and support like righteousness, and some of the radical environmental community is full of it. Strategically, when the perfect becomes the enemy of the good, progress becomes impossible. This is an old problem. Infighting has hampered conservation groups for decades, as Aldo Leopold noted in *A Sand County Almanac* when he wrote, "Conservationists are notorious for their dissensions." Today, the animosity and invective that is poisoning US politics has also infected some of the environmental movement.

Perhaps the best example of this phenomenon is what I call the Nader nadir. If you polled card-carrying environmentalists and asked them to pick their one environmental hero of the last twenty-five years, it would probably be Al Gore. In 2007, he won both an Academy Award for his film, *An Inconvenient Truth,* and shared the Nobel Peace Prize for his work on climate change. No other living US environmental leader has had this level of national and international recognition. Gore's 1992 book *Earth in the Balance: Ecology and the Human Spirit,* written before he became vice president, showed the depth of his understanding of environmental issues. As vice president, he gave environmental leaders unparalleled access to the White House. Even though I worked for a group that leaned more Independent or Republican, I was a part of at least twenty meetings with Gore from 1995 to 2001, including one I arranged with sportsmen leaders. I was part of eight meetings with President Clinton and many more with other high-ranking officials. It was Gore's influence, more than anything, that opened the Clinton White House to environmental issues and concerns.

Given the fact that many environmentalists regard him as our generation's greatest environmental leader, the fact that it was the Green Party that denied Al Gore the presidency should make it clear that a radical ideological approach works against environmentalists' own goals by their own definitions. Even Al Gore was not good enough for Green Party environmentalists in Florida, so they kept him from becoming president. George Bush won the presidency by 537 votes in Florida, where 97,421 people voted for Ralph Nader. If less than one percent of them had changed their vote, Al Gore would have won the election and become the forty-third president of the United States.

Relationships with the best friends within administrations can suffer a similar fate. Christie Todd Whitman became the ninth administrator of the US Environmental Protection Agency on January 31, 2001, appointed by Pres. George W. Bush. She was a fantastic choice for the job but was so badly beaten up by the far right and far left that she lasted only two years before resigning. As the first woman governor of New Jersey and only the second Republican woman governor anywhere, Whitman put together a solid record of conservation achievement. Air quality violations in New Jersey fell from forty-five to four during her two terms. She added one million acres of open-space protection and established watershed management plans to control water pollution. Today, most point sources of pollution actually coming out of factories are pretty well controlled. Most water pollution is caused by run-off from farms, industrial sites, and from air pollution deposited on the land. Whitman was honored by the activist Natural Resources Defense Council for cleaning up New Jersey's waters so effectively that beach closings dropped dramatically during her eight years as governor.

Just before she arrived at EPA, the outgoing Clinton administration had announced a new maximum contaminant level for arsenic in drinking water. The previous allowable level of fifty parts per billion had been in place since 1942. During the Clinton years, new data from the National Academy of Sciences provided a compelling case for a tighter standard. As was too common in the procrastinating Clinton White House, the new rule for lowering the standard to ten parts per billion was not released until the last minute. The EPA administrator is required by the Safe Water Drinking Act to balance the cost of treatment with public health benefits. Like administrators before her, Whitman wanted to take her own look at the data used to make a last-minute rule change that was promulgated by a lame duck president. In exchange for her due diligence, she was excoriated by many of the same environmentalists who had honored her work in New Jersey. It was just too juicy a sound bite: "Bush EPA to allow more arsenic in the drinking water"—even if it was not true. The headlines were everywhere. After a brief review of the data, she affirmed the science and implemented the ten parts per billion standard to be effective on January 1, 2006. It was the same rule on the same implementation date as the Clinton EPA had proposed. The story of her affirming Clinton's new limit on arsenic in drinking water was run as a media footnote, not as the sensational headline that was run during her review of the data used for the standard.

Later that year, EPA completed a review on the science of the impacts from climate change. There were widespread reports of political interference from the White House. In June of 2003, Whitman resigned. She later attributed her departure to a decision from Vice President Dick Cheney's office to allow major upgrades to coal-fired power plants that would extend their operating life without corresponding upgrades to their pollution controls. In the 1970s, new plants were required to have advanced scrubbers, while older power plants were given an exception to new performance standards. This was based on the theory that these plants would go off line in the near future. Thirty years later, these older plants were still operating without modern scrubbers. Whitman resigned rather than defend the administration's position in court.

Just a few months later, the Bush administration's own cost-benefit analysis found that investments in clean air from the Clean Air Act compromise of 1990, led by Pres. George H. W. Bush, saved eight dollars for each dollar in costs. Whitman was on the right side of the issue for both economic, health, and environmental reasons. Her loss as EPA administrator was a loss for all. Two years later, the Bush administration proposed new rules for clean air improvements. Much of the environmental community did not support them (the perfect being the enemy of the good). Some of the dirtier utilities successfully sued that these new rules were unauthorized by existing law. The issue remains in limbo, resulting in less clean air for people and less planning certainty for the industry that provides our electric power.

A similar dynamic often operates within environmental groups, when people often want to be viewed as the most holy defender of the faith, rather than the most effective at making progress. Internecine wrangling and a lack of kindness within the conservation groups also hamper success when thoughtful people are driven away from participation.

My late friend Don Ferris knew better. Born in 1924, Don gave thousands of volunteer hours and tens of thousands of dollars to conservation over his lifetime. Don served as a national director, president, and board chair of the Izaak Walton League for a good part of his adult life. These were hours away from his family, from his passion for trap shooting, and from his delight for golf. As a successful attorney with his own practice, there were many billable hours and thousands of dollars of income foregone. Don gave a great deal to conservation during most of his most professionally productive years.

Don also gave both his legs to his country. In 1945, as a twenty-year-old marine, he hit the beach at Iwo Jima. A few minutes later, a mortar round landed between his legs. Fifteen months of hospitalization later, he came home to the family farm in Ohio on two wooden legs. Don went to college and law school under the GI Bill, started a business, and raised a family. In the late 1960s he took up trap shooting and became one of the best in the United States. Shooting against able-bodied competitors, Don qualified for the Grand American national championship seventeen times. His interest in trapshooting brought him to the Izaak Walton League, where he became a passionate and effective conservation leader and eventually the volunteer board chairman and then president of the Izaak Walton League of America.

Don had the most indefatigable spirit of anyone I have met. Despite the daily adversity he lived with, Don never felt sorry for himself or lost his sense of humor. There was only one phenomenon that could wear through Don's indefatigable spirit—the propensity of some environmentalists to use the same dead-end ideological tactics and self-righteous personal attacks on each other. Over the years, he sadly watched many smart and dedicated conservationists, both professional and volunteers, walk away from personal involvement in conservation because of the tendency within the community to deal with strategic disagreements by personal attack. It causes a drain of talent that conservation cannot afford.

Those of us who spent time for the conservation cause know that honest disagreements are an unavoidable part of policy work, as is exposure to some wacky behavior. The same week in 1999 that some people called me an "Uncle Tom" and asked for my resignation for agreeing to serve on Louisiana-Pacific's corporate board, another person called me "a sniveling left-wing Democrat ideologue" in a letter to the editor of the Izaak Walton League magazine *Outdoor America*. My crime was suggesting that energy efficiency should be a national priority and that drilling for oil in the spectacular Arctic National Wildlife Refuge should be held as a last resort. While we cannot expect our work to be free of controversy, if the only people who get engaged in conservation are ones with rhino skin, we miss the expertise and commitment of many thoughtful and sensitive people. Honest disagreements need to be a part of our work. For the sake of success alone, personal attacks should not be.

David Brooks describes the all or nothing phenomenon in writing about the 2012 presidential election. It describes some environmentalists equally well:

The No. 1 political fantasy in America today, which has inebriated both parties, is the fantasy that the other party will not exist. It is the fantasy that you are about to win a 1932-style victory that will render your opponents powerless.

Every single speech in this election campaign is based on this fantasy. There hasn't been a speech this year that grapples with the real world—that we live in a highly polarized, evenly divided nation and the next president is going to have to try to pass laws in that context.

It's obvious why candidates talk about the glorious programs they'll create if elected. It fires up crowds and defines values. But we shouldn't forget that it's almost entirely make-believe. In the real world, there are almost never ultimate victories, and it is almost never the case (even if you control the White House and Congress) that you get to do what you want.

To succeed in conservation, we need to stop driving people away from a cause that they are inherently predisposed to support. We need an inclusive and collaborative approach that welcomes people and is respectful of differences of opinion, especially on the inexact art of strategy and compromise.

12

Echoes from Dinosaur

The Perils of Compromise

In a democracy, it is not the impeccable correctness of one's original position that counts most in the end. What counts most, in the end, is the quality and clarity of the ultimate compromise.
—Bruce Babbit, former secretary of the Interior

Success is never final, failure is never fatal. Courage is the only thing.
—Winston Churchill

DOWN AMONG THE RED ROCKS and greenery of the deep river canyon, the air was as clear and the colors as intense as I had ever seen. We had made it through the most challenging of the trip's whitewater safely, and we were setting up in a beautiful riverside camp at least twenty-five miles from the nearest road. After huge and noisy winds the first night, the weather was perfect.

I was the most experienced rafter in this group of eighteen friends and family, so I usually "showed the line" by rowing first through the rapids. Now, cold beer in hand, I could relax and enjoy the three days remaining in the trip without worrying about the others bouncing through the rocks and waves in the rapids behind me.

Dinner was in process. The fragrance of an exotic chicken curry mixed with the sweet smell of riverine vegetation and the dry pungency of the sun-baked piñon pine and juniper grassland that started a few feet away from the river's edge. Squeals of delight from four ever-energetic eight- and twelve-year-old girls, who had discovered a safe rock from which to jump into the river, made the scene even more perfect.

We were in the heart of Dinosaur National Monument, home to some of the most beautiful canyons on Earth. Fifty years ago, environmentalists and conservationists came together to save these spectacular canyons from an ill-advised dam proposal. Their efforts set precedents and raised strategic issues that influenced, and haunted, the next half century of public works and parkland conservation.

The fight to save Echo Park, Lodore Canyon, and Split Mountain Canyon was the first time a major federal public works project was stopped solely for a conservation purpose. Unfortunately, the victory came at a cost. As a compromise for protecting these three canyons, Congress approved dams on four other rivers. One of the dams—Glen Canyon—buried what may have been the most beautiful canyon on earth. The fight to save three canyons in Dinosaur National Monument raised the issue of when and how to compromise. Fifty years later, it's an issue that's still being debated and has not been resolved.

Dinosaur National Monument was established by Pres. Woodrow Wilson in 1915. It straddles the Green River along the northern part of the border between Colorado and Utah, just south of the Wyoming state line. The Green River is the Colorado River's largest tributary. It flows from its source in the high country of Wyoming's Wind River Range to its confluence with the Colorado River in Canyonlands National Park in southeastern Utah. In 1869, John Wesley Powell began his epic journey to explore and map the Grand Canyon country on the Green River. He started just a few miles north of where thousands of recreational rafters now begin their trips.

The core of Dinosaur National Monument is the forty-five-mile canyon that the Green River cuts through the Uinta Mountains. The area features wonderful wilderness camping, exciting whitewater, extraordinary wildlife, ancient Indian cultural sites, and some of the best dinosaur fossil resources in the United States. In the mid-1940s, the US Bureau of Reclamation proposed construction of five major dam projects in the Upper Colorado watershed. One of the projects, consisting of two dams, was proposed for the Green River in Dinosaur National Monument. Back in 1915, President Wilson had set aside this monument to protect the rich dinosaur fossils that were discovered there. The scenic canyons were a bonus. In 1938, Pres. Franklin Roosevelt expanded the park to its present 211,000 acres to protect the canyon country along the Green and Yampa Rivers.

In the late 1940s, Americans using World War II surplus rafts discovered the world-class scenery and wildlife in the river canyons. Today, it is one of the nation's most popular float trips. The proposed dams would have flooded all of the canyons in Dinosaur—the breathtaking Lodore and Split Mountain Canyons, all of the Yampa River Canyons, and the awesome Echo Park, where the two rivers join.

The proposal to build these dams became a national cause almost immediately. This was the first time a major dam-building project was proposed in a national park unit. Conservationists felt that allowing a dam to be built there would set a bad precedent for other national parks. At the time, dams were also being considered to flood portions of Glacier, Mammoth Cave, and Kings Canyon National Parks. Even the Grand Canyon itself faced a serious threat from dams. Many parks faced other types of development proposals, causing some conservationists to question the future of the national park system itself. The stakes were high.

From the time our nation was formed to our bicentennial, we built seventy-five thousand dams—an average of one per day for over two hundred years. Many of these facilities brought us only the illusion of progress. We have inundated six hundred thousand miles of streams and rivers and destroyed hundreds of thousands of acres of wildlife habitat. We lost great runs of migratory fish, eliminated some fish species totally, increased salinity, degraded water quality, increased evaporative water loss, and destroyed wetlands. We have spent billions to remove dams, repair waterways, or clean up and rebuild after dam failures. We will spend trillions more as the massive dams built during the middle of the twentieth century become full of silt and need to be dredged or removed.

The dam-building era in the United States is now over. Dams provide immediate benefits but leave a footprint of ecological impacts that can take hundreds of years to erase. Decommissioning dams will require governments to spend billions of dollars to fix problems that were never anticipated. The Association of State Dam Safety Officials says that the cost of upgrading or repairing all of our nation's non-federal dams alone would exceed thirty-six billion dollars. Ill-conceived dams borrow from the future. They provide low-cost power and water to today's generation; however, they saddle future generations with untold long-term costs.

The fight to stop the Echo Park Dam project was the first time that hiking and climbing groups like the Sierra Club and National Parks Conservation Association came together with hunting and fishing groups like the Izaak Walton League. Recognizing the extraordinary wildlife resource at stake, the firearms-industry-funded Wildlife Management Institute also joined the effort.

At this one place and time, these groups bridged the historic gulf between the preservationist philosophy of John Muir, the Sierra Club's founder, and the pro-management philosophy of Gifford Pinchot, the first US Forest Service chief. The preservation-versus-management debate that these two conservation giants started almost a century ago continues to this day, to some extent distinguishing conservationists from environmentalists.

In this case, the results of their unified efforts were stunning. There were extensive congressional hearings, large public debates, and substantial media coverage of the fight over this little-known park. Until that time, no conservation issue had ever attracted that kind of attention. This was the first, and one of the only moments ever, at which the sportsmen conservation community and the environmental movement emerged as a unified force in national politics.

"In their fight to save Dinosaur National Monument, conservationists demonstrated an unprecedented solidarity, an adeptness at lobbying, and a heightened awareness of the economic and technical arguments that had been used so long by the opposition," says Jon M. Cosco, author of *Echo Park, Struggle for Preservation*. "By coming together, they gained a political voice." From the beginning, the Izaak Walton League's Joe Penfold and Bill Vogt were at the forefront of the effort to stop the dam. The Sierra Club's charismatic leader, David Brower, was a relative newcomer to the fight but grabbed most of the headlines and credit for the victory. Ironically, he would later call the compromise the greatest mistake of his life.

On April 11, 1956, Pres. Dwight D. Eisenhower signed a compromise public works bill allowing four storage dams in the Upper Colorado River drainage. This included the Curecanti Dam on the Gunnison River in Colorado, Flaming Gorge Dam on the Green River in Wyoming, the Navajo Dam on the San Juan River in New Mexico, and the Glen Canyon Dam on the main stem Colorado River in Arizona. After fifteen years of effort, the Echo Park Dam in Dinosaur National Monument was permanently removed from the project.

Conservationists soon realized that the compromise had cost them an even bigger prize—the extraordinary network of slickrock canyons, slot canyons, glades, and glens that comprised the Glen Canyon of the Colorado. The euphoria of conservation's greatest victory to date quickly faded. None of the other four dams allowed under the plan were located in a national park or monument, so they had received less attention during the debate. Soon after the compromise was struck, glowing reports started coming in from visitors to the little known

Glen Canyon, which is just upriver from the Grand Canyon. The Glen Canyon Dam was the largest of the dams approved under the compromise and the only one on the main stem of the Colorado.

By 1990, when the Glen Canyon Dam was finally full, it buried hundreds of miles of canyon country. Early visitors, including the legendary photographer Eliot Porter, writer Ed Abbey, and artist Georgia O'Keefe, declared it at least as beautiful as the Grand Canyon and maybe the most beautiful canyon on Earth. Today, the Sierra Club and others have called for removal of the dam, and the Glen Canyon Institute exists primarily to encourage that idea.

The fight for Echo Park presented conservationists with an excruciating strategic decision, much like the ones that now dominate our daily work. The issues of when to negotiate and compromise became extremely controversial. In saving Echo Park, Lodore Canyon, Split Mountain Canyon, and the Yampa River Canyons in Dinosaur National Park, conservationists set a precedent that protected many other parks. In the process, we lost another place of equal or greater beauty. Those conservationists forged the best deal possible under the conditions of their time. Had they not done so, would Glen Canyon be saved today? Or would Echo Park and maybe parts of Glacier National Park and Grand Canyon National Park also be flooded and lost?

With each passing day during our trip on the river, I watched the pure joy of our children and their natural ease in a wilderness setting. I saw the maturing of teenagers, the deepening contentment of the adults, and the building of *plein-air* friendships. The scene is repeated throughout our national parks millions of times each year. The National Park Service manages 392 units, 58 of which are national parks. The others are national monuments, lakeshores, seashores, historic sites, heritage areas, and other sites. Over 280 million people enter a park each year.

Each year, about 15,000 thousand people will float through the canyons of Dinosaur National Monument, experiencing a spiritual rejuvenation, building friendships with others, learning self-reliance, and reconnecting with the natural world. Most will have no idea why this place remains. We will need those friendships if we are to protect these special places in the future.

The issue of when and how to compromise is the most hotly debated issue in conservation. The fight to save the canyons of Dinosaur National Monument stopped an ill-conceived dam project. It established a precedent that has kept major public works projects out of national parks for over fifty years. Like all victories, however, it was an imperfect one. The national parks may be America's best idea. An active broad base of support will do the best job in assuring they are viable for future generations to enjoy them as we have.

As our trip ended, we felt the usual ambivalence of leaving the sylvan fellowship of the past week to the comfort of a hot shower and soft bed. I thought about the 1953 raft trip where Joe Penfold, the Izaak Walton League's western representative, and two powerful members of Congress floated the river together and agreed this place should be protected. I regretted the loss of Glen Canyon but wondered if anything could have been done in that era to prevent it. Did the compromise save at least this gem that we had enjoyed together over the past few days? Years after the compromise, when Utah senators asked the powerful Colorado Rep. Wayne Aspinall to renew the fight to build a dam in Echo Park, he replied, "We have an agreement with the conservationists, and it will be honored." It is that kind of good faith, more than anything, that will give us the ability to steer the earth toward our children's future.

Seeing the Fiscal Forest through the Trees

Conservation Spending and the National Debt

Arithmetic is not an opinion.
—Italian proverb

My involvement in this issue has allowed me
to piss off just about everyone in America.
—former Senator Alan Simpson, co-chair of the President's
Commission on Fiscal Responsibility and Reform

A s with environmental sustainability, fiscal sustainability is also a neighborly vision that asks how we can live together without hurting each other today or stealing the future from our children. Our nation is on an unsustainable fiscal path, requiring the government to borrow huge sums each year. Addressing this crisis will require cuts in both annual domestic and defense spending, significant changes in the big entitlement programs, and tax reform that simplifies the code and generates additional revenue. It should be clear to all that everything must be on the table—spending cuts and tax reform that generates more revenue.

In fiscal year 2011, federal spending was $3.6 trillion, revenue was $2.3 trillion, and the deficit was $1.3 trillion. As of June 1, 2013, the gross national debt, the accumulation of years of deficits, is now $17 trillion.

Of that, $11.5 trillion is publicly held—over half by foreign interests. Interest on the publicly held debt was $224 billion last year but is estimated to swell to over $1 trillion by 2022 under the Concord Coalition's plausible scenario for future deficits as interest rates rise back to more typical historic averages of 5–6 percent. For the first time since World War II, the gross debt now exceeds the gross domestic product and is projected to be almost three times GDP by 2038.

According to the Treasury Department's 2011 Financial Report of the United States, the public debt and unfunded future obligations—including Social Security, Medicare, and federal pensions—now exceed $57 trillion. This is roughly equal to the net worth of all Americans. Others estimate this unfunded liability to be over $70 trillion. With continued trillion-dollar-plus deficits projected even after a full economic recovery, our fiscal situation is not sustainable. Former chair of the Joint Chiefs Adm. Mike Mullen calls this "the greatest threat to our national security."

Structural deficits in Medicare, Medicaid, Social Security, and over two hundred "tax expenditures"—special interest tax breaks such as deferrals, exclusions, exemptions, deductions, preferential rates, and credits—must be reformed to improve economic efficiency, broaden the tax base, and reduce the gap between spending and revenue. These tax expenditures and entitlement programs are projected to grow rapidly.

By contrast, in fiscal year 2011, cutting all of the $650 billion in domestic annual spending, twice over, would have been needed to balance spending and revenue. Spending cuts in the annual domestic budgets alone cannot solve the nation's fiscal crisis. Due to cuts made by the Budget Control Act of 2011, domestic and military spending are not projected to grow beyond inflation.

Unfortunately, many elected officials have long focused on only one part of the federal budget: the "discretionary" domestic spending programs that Congress approves each year. Instead of taking a comprehensive approach to fiscal reform, they keep coming back to the same places to look for more and more savings—and they never get the larger deficit-reduction job done. Meanwhile, some popular programs that involve what most people consider basic government programs have been disproportionately targeted for cuts, producing inefficiencies, lost opportunities, public frustration, and poor long-term policies.

Funding for popular natural resource conservation programs provides a telling example. Cost-effective wildlife and natural resource conservation is a critical concept that receives great lip service in Washington but often comes up short when it comes to actual policy. These are programs that create almost ten million jobs and generate over one hundred billion dollars in federal, state, and local tax revenue. They leverage billions of additional dollars per year in private investment.

The portion of the federal budget that covers all environmental and natural resource funding, called Function 300, has been cut substantially in recent decades. In 1982, almost 4 percent of federal spending went to these programs. In 2012, this line item received less than 1 percent, just thirty-five billion dollars. By comparison, tax expenditures—credits, exemptions, deferrals, and other breaks given to specific groups in the tax code—now cost America $1.3 trillion per year. In other words, these tax expenditures cost the nation thirty-seven times more than the entire amount each year spent on all environment and natural resource programs.

Spending on fish, wildlife, and natural resources—of most concern to hunters, anglers, and other wildlife conservation groups—is now only 0.4 percent of the federal budget. Deeper cuts have been proposed, including the complete elimination of funding for the North American Wetland Conservation Act and the Land and Water Conservation Fund. This is out of step with what most Americans expect from their government.

A 2012 poll by the bipartisan research team of Fairbank, Maslin, Maullin, Metz & Associates (D) and Public Opinion Strategies (R) found that three-quarters of Americans say that even with federal budget problems, funding for conservation should *not* be cut. Fully 74 percent agree that "even with federal budget problems, funding to safeguard land, air and water should not be cut," including a majority of voters across the partisan spectrum and two-thirds or greater in every region of the country.

Voters say they are willing to back up this belief. Fully 83 percent are willing to pay additional taxes to protect US land, water, and wildlife. When provided with a range of dollar amounts to pay in increased taxes, the vast majority of voters are willing to pay some amount more, including 72 percent of Tea Party Republicans, 73 percent of self-described conservatives, 88 percent of moderates, and 94 percent of self-described liberals.

While there must be shared sacrifice if we are to stabilize the nation's debt and build a sound foundation for economic growth, additional cuts to highly leveraged and cost-effective programs such as natural resource conservation cannot have a meaningful impact on the deficit.

American taxes are not sufficient to pay for the programs that many people want, like Medicare, Social Security, road construction, and education subsidies. This is a basic problem for democracies: people tend to vote for politicians who promise more and provide more than we are willing to pay for. Approving tax cuts and spending increases are always easier to do than figuring out how to pay for them. In 2012, 15 percent of Americans live in poverty. The share of Americans in extreme poverty—with an income less than half the poverty line—is the highest in the thirty-five years of Census Bureau records. No nation is strong enough to carry large pockets of unproductive people. The global economy requires education for jobs, which requires investments in education.

Most independent economists agree that we cannot cut, tax, or grow our way out of this—we must do all three. This is the fundamental conclusion of every responsible group that has examined the issue, most prominently the Simpson-Bowles commission. There is no credible path to deficit reduction without a combination of spending cuts and revenue increases. In thirty polls conducted over the past year Americans agree with this by a margin of at least 2 to 1. Everything must be on the table. There must be shared sacrifice. If there is stimulus, it should be "timely, targeted, and temporary" as the Concord Coalition calls for.

In their Moment of Truth report, Alan Simpson and Erskine Bowles state, "Every modest sacrifice we refuse to make today only forces greater sacrifices of hope and opportunity upon the next generation." We face a simple reality: to fund the needs of an aging America while also investing in the future means we'll all have to cut spending and pay a little more. The best way to do that is to simplify the tax code, removing the plethora of credits, deductions, deferrals, and other carve-outs, in order to lower federal spending and raise revenue.

Finally and most importantly, however, both fiscal and environmental sustainability are about our children's future. When we do not balance spending and revenue, we are simply stealing the future from them. Those elected leaders who refuse to compromise are, effectively, advocates for the United States to fail. Politics can be an organization of hatreds or the art of the possible. As writer Tom Friedman puts it, "As a nation, we have to do something hard, we have to do it now, and we have to do it together." Environmental and fiscal sustainability go hand in hand. Both require good faith engagement and compromise to succeed.

14

Rules of Engagement

Making Collaboration Real

*Coming together is a beginning. Keeping together
is progress. Working together is success.*
—Henry Ford

*Recreational development is a job not of building roads into lovely country,
but of building receptivity into the still unlovely human mind.*
—Aldo Leopold

OFFERING THE NOSTRUM that people should work together is a staple in conservation speeches, especially in the natural resources profession and most especially with government employees. Making it happen is never easy. Participation without an open mind almost assures failure. The greatest progress killers are bad-faith engagements. Honesty, respect, and a measure of humility from both sides are key to success.

On a beautiful spring day in 2002 when Washington, DC, dripped with cherry blossoms, the two top executives of the powerful forest products industry trade association, the American Forest and Paper Association, quietly took me to an off-the-record lunch. They wanted to thank me for six years of "tough love" as they called it. It had been a difficult process, so it was best for all of us to do this privately. I had been an outsider invited to be deeply involved in their trade association's business—working to improve forestry standards for an entire industry in a way that put the greatest pressure on the poorest performers.

Trade associations, like some environmental groups, tend to be run by those who feel most passionate about the issues and are least likely to think strategically or be willing to compromise. Even though we would have preferred to take the industry even further toward sustainability, it was remarkable how far we had come. While far from perfect, no other major resource extraction industry has ever come close to establishing as comprehensive a set of standards as the dual certification systems the forest products industry now operates under. The process had never been easy, but I was convinced that these leaders' interest in progress had always been real. There had been trust and respect between us, even though we did not always agree. We had moved an industry to a higher standard, too far for some and not far enough for other. We made progress, but not everyone within the industry or the environmental community was pleased with us.

Trust and respect is essential to durable progress in conservation. Engagement between interests needs to be real and honest. Mistrust lasts for years and is a major killer of progress. It is the most common excuse for failure to engage. In an era where compromise is often viewed as cowardice and kindness is seen as weakness, those willing to engage with their opponents can pay a high price. Conservation executives, even CEOs, have lost jobs due to their willingness to reach out and come to the table. Others have spent tedious days, months, or years on a collaborative process, only to find the process was not in good faith and was put forward only as a diversion. This can be devastating when the conservation leader who was willing to reach out is already under scrutiny, suspicion, or even public condemnation by other conservationists for their participation. When it comes to collaboration, both sides have made costly mistakes.

Mike Furtman is a self-employed outdoor writer, so when he was asked to be part of a multi-stakeholder effort to try to break the grid-lock on timber management in northern Minnesota in 1995, he knew that participating was going to cost him money. Mike had authored several popular outdoor books and is a sought-after writer, but free-lance writing is a tough way to make a living in the best of times. He also knew that participating would make him a target, especially if the effort was successful. Any compromise would not be popular with one side or the other, and those were people who bought his books on the North Country. Progress was tedious, but almost a year into the process they were on the verge of an agreement that everyone could live with. It would be a long-awaited win-win for the northern forests. Key to the agreement was the size of the streamside management zones, the buffer where timber cutting would not be allowed. At the eleventh hour, the representatives from the Boise Cascade forest products company changed their minds and pulled support for the agreement that everyone had spent a year working on and had agreed to. Mike had nothing to show for a full year of effort, including hundreds of hours of meetings, long drives, and preparation. He was out about twenty-five thousand dollars in lost freelance work.

Ted Roosevelt IV points to a situation where Montana ranchers agreed to designated wilderness protection for an area, the highest level of public land protection. They did so based on assurances that legal grazing would not be opposed, only to have their grazing allotments challenged by environmentalists soon after the bill passed.

Most tragic are the times when both sides manage to find a compromise but find themselves overruled by politics. The Selway-Salmon-Bitterroot Ecosystem is the largest block of wilderness habitat remaining in the lower forty-eight United States. Of all remaining un-occupied grizzly bear habitat in the lower forty-eight states, this area has the best potential to support a healthy population of grizzly bears and to boost long-term survival and recovery prospects for this species. In 1995 the US Fish and Wildlife Service began a multi-stakeholder process with the idea of reintroducing an "experimental" population of grizzly bears. An experimental population would provide exceptions to Endangered Species Act protection by allowing for more bear management and removal of problem bears. After five years of effort, an extraordinary compromise was forged with local landowners, timber companies, environmentalists, and hunters on one of the West's most difficult issues. Key to the compromise was the establishment of a Citizen Management Committee of diverse interests that gave local interests unprecedented control of the reintroduction and management decisions going forward. The compromise announced on November 17, 2000, in the Record of Decision was supported by strong majorities in the region and nationwide. It allowed grizzly bears to be reintroduced under these special rules and restrictions. Seven months later, the decision was unilaterally rescinded by the new administration of George W. Bush.

Holding elected officials accountable for decisions like this is a difficult task. For six years, 1996–2002, I was on the board of the League of Conservation Voters. LCV publishes a National Environmental Scorecard to inform the public about the most important environmental legislation of the past congressional session and show how their representatives voted. It is an important role. For example, in 1990, after the bipartisan passage of the Clean Air Act reauthorization and acid rain controls, Minnesota Senator Rudy Boschwitz came home to campaign on the fact that he had voted for the Clean Air Act. In fact, he voted against the bill many times, trying to weaken it. When the final outcome was a foregone conclusion, he voted for final passage so he could come home and make the fatuous claim that he supported clean air. By documenting voting records on the real votes that decide issues, LCV tries to bring transparency to false political claims like Boschwitz's.

For accountability like this to be effective it needs to be fair, and LCV has occasionally fallen short. Congress passed into law the Shark

Finning Prohibition Act of 2000 to prohibit the repulsive practice of catching a shark, cutting off the fins, and returning the remainder of the shark to the sea to die. Wanton waste like this is never acceptable to hunters, and it should not be to commercial fishermen. The environmental community and others had pushed for this bill, and a strong majority of the members of Congress, but not all, stepped forward to pass it. I proposed to have this vote included on the LCV National Environmental Scorecard but was outvoted because "too many Republicans voted for it." That year, knowing full well that the vast majority of the Congress voted in favor of ending this egregious practice, LCV promoted the "fact" that many members of Congress got a zero score on environmental issues. They got a zero only because LCV did not count the vote to end a horrible practice that all of the environmental community opposed and that most of the Congress had voted for. During the same time, LCV reversed votes in favor of endorsing Republican candidates who had broken ranks with their party and voted for conservation. This combination of events resulted in the resignation of LCV's only Republican staff member and three out of four Republican board members—one of whom was the LCV board chair, a former state governor, and former assistant secretary of the Interior for Fish, Wildlife and Parks. I finished my second three-year term but did not seek a third term. I had lost faith in the integrity of the process. The environmental community cannot have an accountability function whereby Democrats tell Democrats to vote for Democrats and have it play a meaningful or effective role. There needs to be a fairly applied process for bringing much needed transparency to the political process.

Robert Craig founded the Keystone Center in 1975 to provide a place and a structure for problem solving on conservation and other issues. Keystone looks for stakeholders who have become frustrated with the traditional adversarial process and are willing to try a different approach to sit in council on a tough issue and address it in a disciplined manner. The Keystone Center has a thirty-five-year history of serving as an independent convener and facilitator of cross-sector groups who are differently positioned on important public policy issues. They base their work on independence and neutrality; the use of the best scientific and technical information available to help inform policy solutions; having different stakeholder perspectives represented; and a knack for engaging those stakeholders in creating well-informed, practical solutions to tough problems. Keystone has successfully organized and facilitated stakeholder deliberations on sustainable forestry, forest health, roadless area protection, air pollution, endangered species, marine mammal protection, chemical weapons, mountaintop coal mining, and hydropower relicensing. I served on Keystone's board and think that its approach holds great promise in these divisive times.

Often, multi-stakeholder processes have volunteer conservationists at the table with paid employees from industry. It is already not a fair fight. It is nearly impossible for volunteers to be able to make the same time commitment as paid employees. Even if they have great expertise, they rarely have staff behind them to assist with research and the crafting of position statements. A structured process, like the one used by Keystone, can level the playing field and build confidence in the outcome. This small nonprofit organization has been able to bring together people to forge agreements on green product certification, endangered species, nuclear energy, sustainable agriculture, climate change, clean energy, biotechnology, transportation, and urban planning. Keystone also assists company advisory panels of outside stakeholders by providing a third-party neutral facilitator.

Well-constructed processes for engagement have great promise to improve conservation outcomes across the landscape of issues. Much has been written and practiced on conflict resolution: identifying stakeholders, screening out people with immovable agendas, clarifying issues, focusing on common values, and building relationships. Process alone, however, cannot assure success. Unless a process yields durable results and action on the ground, we have wasted our time. Worse, we may have lost the precious opportunity for building the trust on which progress depends. To succeed in conservation, we must also "build receptivity into the still unlovely human mind" as Aldo Leopold wrote in his classic *A Sand County Almanac* in 1948. We cannot succeed without engaging beyond our own circle of allies.

15

Infinite Harm

If We Fail

*In myriad ways humanity is linked to the millions of other species on the planet.
What concerns them, concerns us. The more we ignore our common health and
welfare, the greater are the many threats to our own species. The better we
understand and the more we rationally manage our relationship to the rest
of life, the greater the guarantee of our own safety and quality of life.*
—Edward O. Wilson, Harvard professor, Pulitzer Prize winner

Conservation is a test. If we pass we might get to keep the planet.
—Marjory Stoneman Douglas, Florida conservationist

M ANY OF THE EARTH's most distinguished scientists are pessimistic that we humans have any long-term future at all. "Natural systems that support economies, lives and livelihoods across the planet are at risk of rapid degradation and collapse, unless there is swift, radical and creative action to conserve and sustainably use the variety of life on Earth." That is the principal conclusion of the 2010 Global Biodiversity Outlook, produced by the United Nation's Environment Program. The report confirms that the world has failed to meet its target to achieve a significant reduction in the rate of biodiversity loss. It highlights the fact that outreach and engagement are the keys to success: "A key lesson from the failure to meet the 2010 biodiversity target is that the urgency of a change of direction must be conveyed to decision makers beyond the constituency so far involved in the biodiversity convention." In other words, outreach is key.

The Global Biodiversity Outlook uses multiple lines of evidence to demonstrate that the target set by world governments in 2002 "to achieve by 2010 a significant reduction of the current rate of biodiversity loss at the global, regional and national level" has not been met. Based on a special analysis of biodiversity indicators carried out by a panel of scientists, as well as peer-reviewed scientific literature and reports from national governments to the CBD, key findings include:

- None of the twenty-one subsidiary targets accompanying the overall 2010 biodiversity target can be said definitively to have been achieved globally, although some have been partially or locally achieved. Ten of fifteen headline indicators developed by the CBD show trends unfavorable for biodiversity.
- No government claims to have completely met the 2010 biodiversity target at the national level, and around one-fifth state explicitly that it has not been met.
- Species that have been assessed for extinction risk are on average moving closer to extinction, with amphibians facing the greatest risk and coral species deteriorating most rapidly in status.
- The abundance of vertebrate species, based on assessed populations, fell by nearly one-third on average between 1970 and 2006 and continues to fall globally, with especially severe declines in the tropics and among freshwater species.
- Natural habitats in most parts of the world continue to decline in extent and integrity, notably freshwater wetlands, sea ice habitats, salt marshes, coral reefs, seagrass beds, and shellfish reefs, although there has been significant progress in slowing the rate of loss of tropical forests and mangroves, in some regions.
- Crop and livestock genetic diversity continues to decline in agricultural systems. For example, more than sixty breeds of livestock are reported to have become extinct since 2000.

- The five principal pressures directly driving biodiversity loss (habitat change, overexploitation, pollution, invasive alien species, and climate change) are either constant or increasing in intensity.
- There has been significant progress in the increase of protected areas both on land and in coastal waters. However, 44 percent of terrestrial eco-regions (areas with a large proportion of shared species and habitat types) and 82 percent of marine eco-regions fall below the target of 10 percent protection. The majority of sites judged to be of special importance to biodiversity also fall outside protected areas.

By any measure, the carrying capacity of the earth cannot support even today's human population at the average income lifestyle in the developed world. By some estimates, it would take the natural resources of four more planet earths to be able to do that. By any sampling, there should be more than enough indicators of our need for more successful environmental policy. Oberlin College professor David Orr and others point to some of these indicators.

- Half of all wetlands in the United States are gone, including some of the most biologically productive acres on earth. We are still losing about one hundred thousand acres per year.
- Male sperm counts have fallen by 50 percent since the 1930s, and no one really knows why. We are truly not the same men our grandfathers were.
- Two million acres of natural habitat per year are lost in the United States.
- Available agricultural land has declined from 1.2 acres per person in the 1960s to about 0.5 acres per person in 2005.
- Populations of amphibians worldwide have declined precipitously, and no one knows why.
- Species of fungi and bacteria that decay plant material and recycle nutrients are being lost before we even know they are there and how they work.

- Water shortages and overdrawn aquifers already limit crucial supplies to billions of people.
- Extinction rates are about one hundred times natural baseline trends.
- World population continues to grow by about 250,000 per day. The growth is especially strong in countries that can least afford it.

"We are near a tipping point, a point of no return, beyond which the built-in momentum and feedbacks will carry us to levels of climate change with staggering consequences for humanity," says NASA climate scientist Dr. James Hansen. In 2007, Dr. Rajendra Pachauri, chair of the Intergovernmental Panel on Climate Change, warned the world: "What we do in the next two to three years will determine our future. This is the defining moment."

It is easy to understand environmentalists' sense of urgency and frustration with the lack of progress being made on pressing conservation issues—many of which have compelling solutions at hand. They have intimate knowledge of what has already been lost. Whole ecosystems have disintegrated. Once-abundant species are gone altogether. Most of us carry body burdens of toxic substances in our flesh. Some species, such as beluga whales in Quebec's St. Lawrence River, are so laden with bio-accumulated toxins that their cadavers must be treated as toxic waste. Air and water quality have improved in a few areas but remain seriously degraded in others. The blue oceans are dying, especially in the biological nurseries of coral reefs and estuaries. By most estimates, there will be no coral reefs in fifty years due to increased ocean temperature and acidity. Habitat loss of all kinds is widespread. Worst of all, climate change exacerbates all of these problems and presents us with an unprecedented threat to all life.

By most measures, environmental awareness continued to improve from 1990 to 2010. During the same time period, collective action did not improve, and federal spending did not improve. The portion of the

US federal budget that includes all spending on conservation and natural resources is called Function 300. Prior to 1984, Function 300 accounted for 4 percent of the nation's budget. Today it is less than 1 percent.

Individual action is not the solution. It cannot be a substitute for collective action. I drive a hybrid car, garden, compost, super-insulated my home, use energy-efficient lights and appliances, hunt for our meat, and try to buy locally. I have no illusion that these activities will mean much until they are standard practices for all. Individual action is important leadership by example, but even though 90 percent of us claim we recycle and buy green products, we are producing 35 percent more garbage than we did on Earth Day 1970. We cannot buy or recycle our way to an environmentally sustainable future.

We can succeed in conservation, and much else, if Americans begin to reject the ferocity of brain-dead partisans. They are a small minority whose impact is overblown by stridency-obsessed news talkers and anonymous bloggers. Hyperbolic rants are worse than useless; they are destructive to the fabric of our civil society and our future. They are destructive to our environment. If Americans return to their ruthlessly pragmatic commonsense selves and the tradition of civility, and insist on that from our leaders, we can succeed in protecting the environment. Only solutions that gain board and diverse support make it through the complex system of checks and balances that is our democratic government. We simply cannot succeed without bringing people together.

The Ten Convenient Truths
of Conservation Success

*Despite nearly a century of propaganda, conservation still proceeds at a snail's
pace: progress still consists largely of letterhead pieties and convention oratory. On
the back forty we still slip two steps backward for each forward stride.*
—Aldo Leopold, *A Sand County Almanac*

*There is only so much time and so many resources, and there is so much
work to be done. There are also true believers who are dedicated to a cause
where success, failure, and results are irrelevant, and we need such people.
They are our conscience. But very few of them achieve. Maybe
their rewards are in Heaven. But that's not sure, either.*
—Peter Drucker

I N THIS BOOK, I AM NOT ADVOCATING for a diminishment in the
level of environmental protection to which we aspire. I am advocating for an efficiently protective and sustainable future. I want conservation success, and think the next generation needs to adopt a smarter
and more inclusive way of reaching our goal of saving the planet. I
think the evidence shows that it provides the most likely avenue for
success.

There are indications that the next generation of leaders is on their
way. Support for a greener society is highest among youth of all races
and classes, and they are much savvier than many senior environmental leaders on the need to align environment and business interests and
concerns. They are already more tolerant than their elders on issues of
race, religion, nationality, and sexual orientation. They are less toler-

ant of incivility: the "gotcha" politics and demonizing gridlock that is rapidly destroying our nation. They see gridlock, correctly, as a great threat to our nation that affects our ability to deliver on all issues. They understand that the impairment of our democracy by harsh polarization presents a greater threat than any foreign adversary. The current political dynamic makes us as a nation incapable of protecting the environment, balancing the budget, defending our homeland, or assuring a future for coming generations. "We have met the enemy, and he is us," as the comic strip *Pogo* warned us years ago.

Most young people get it. It is time to disarm. We need more mediators and fewer gladiators. Conservation is not a contest that will be decided by a partisan victory when one party or group finally has all the marbles. Especially in the case of widely supported issues like conservation, partisanship equals paralysis. All of the periods of major progress in history have come when Republicans and Democrats worked together. This is true for all of the major success in conservation: the great land-protection initiatives of Pres. Theodore Roosevelt, the pollution control infrastructure and laws of Presidents Richard Nixon and Gerald Ford, and the ozone depletion and air pollution breakthroughs during the end the of term of Pres. Ronald Reagan and the George H. W. Bush administration. In US history, there has been no major victory for the environment that was not forged by bipartisan compromise. It is unlikely there ever will be. Both sides of the political divide need to be part of the solution.

Unfortunately, a majority of young people is estranged from the political process, and most of them do not even vote. In 2008, only 49 percent of eligible eighteen- to twenty-eight-year-old people voted. Seventy percent of those over age 45 went to the polls. I struggle on how to discuss this with young people without coming off as a finger-wagging geezer. Their lack of participation impairs their future most of all. I understand their frustration but not their lack of participation in the electoral process.

When media punditry oversimplifies any issue, progress is made much more difficult. As veteran television journalist Ted Koppel said, when we seek "a flood of opinions designed to confirm our own bias, the trend is not good for the republic." For many pundits, the world is black and white. They are beholden to fringe elements, to getting attention for themselves, and to placating their base—not to making progress. The real world is more nuanced. Gray is the color of truth. The practical middle, where most of us live, gets less emphasis in the "infotainment" media debate because it is less entertaining, even though that is how most Americans identify themselves. The major polls now find that more Americans identify themselves as Independents than Republicans or Democrats. Today, about 40 percent call themselves moderate rather than liberal or conservative. Yet, with much of the media, if you do not have a doctrinaire view and a big mouth, you do not get a voice. The approval rating for Congress hovers around 15 percent and goes down as polarization increases. The approval rate for political parties is even lower.

To behave ethically is to be engaged effectively in protecting the earth for future generations and the creatures with which we share the earth. To be engaged ethically means being engaged effectively, means working with others. Outreach is key, but most professional environmentalists spend much more time meeting with each other than they do meeting with adversaries, swing votes, or potential allies. Even their meetings with supporters are often aimed more at entertainment and self-affirmation than information. Our prospects for success are inextricably tied to the broadness of the base of support for an issue, yet our organizations are becoming much more insular. In 1974, when I first became involved in conservation there were about one hundred conservation organizations. Today there are about ten thousand. Too much of the money generously donated to many of these groups ends up being spent on duplicative, internecine, or futile efforts. Gathering with others that already think like you may feel better and be more self-reinforcing, but reaching out to others is what gets things done.

That is where progress occurs. Most of our great issues can be resolved not with a yes or no but with a discussion of how—conducted by diverse groups of people in good faith.

For about 1/1000 of the world's gross domestic product, a fraction of what was summoned up instantly by the world's governments in 2008–2009 to avoid an economic meltdown, the world could avoid a much more serious and irreversible environmental catastrophe. Worldwide, for the cost of the subsidies for extractive industries alone, we could pay for the cost of necessary ecological protection. There are many examples in which environmental improvements have, contrary to popular expectation, been highly cost-effective. As the Deepwater Horizon and other "accidents" showed us, prevention is key. Once the genie is out of the bottle, there is no putting her back. Anti-government and anti-regulatory fervor guarantees that more corners will be cut and "accidents" will occur. Poorly written laws and too many lawsuits drive people away from the rules any society needs in order to survive. Long-term wealth is contingent on keeping the planet healthy and avoiding these catastrophes.

In fact, healthy economies are always the best for the environment. Countries, and states, with the best environmental records also have the best economies. Gold and Green 2000, a report by the Institute for Southern Studies, used two separate lists of indicators to evaluate each state's economic and environmental performance. The twenty economic indicators include annual pay, job opportunities, business start-ups, and workplace injury rates. The twenty environmental measures range from toxic emissions and pesticide use to energy consumption and urban sprawl. Comparing the two lists reveals very positive correlations between economic and environmental performance. Seven states rank in the top fifteen for both economic and environmental health. Vermont, Rhode Island, and Minnesota rank in the top six on both lists, with Colorado, Maryland, Maine, and Wisconsin in the top fifteen on both. By contrast, ten states are among the worst fifteen on both lists, including Alabama, Texas, Tennessee, Mississippi, Indiana,

Arkansas, West Virginia, Kentucky, and South Carolina. Even before Katrina and Deepwater Horizon, Louisiana ranked forty-eighth on economic performance and fiftieth on the environment.

Conservation efforts require coalitions and compromise. Groups whom we have identified as "not us" may, in fact, share some core concerns with us. We can get to a similar place without having to agree with every one of each other's reasons for going there. We need to listen to people with diverse opinions in order to find out what values we have in common and then be willing to compromise in order to form alliances. We must resist the urge to view compromise as "selling out."

Human rights leader and environmentalist Van Jones describes what he calls the Noah principles:

1. Fewer "issues," more solutions.
2. Fewer "demands," more goals.
3. Fewer "targets," more partners.
4. Less "accusation," more confession.
5. Less "cheap patriotism," more deep patriotism.

To succeed, conservation needs more friends and fewer enemies. Too often, environmentalists' tactics create more opposition than support. We need to take a lesson from the civil rights movement. They did not start by demanding that an African American be president. They engaged and moved a nation and a people strategically and inspirationally from voting rights to integrated buses and sports, to legalization of interracial marriage, to a nation where a man who happens to be African American can become president because a majority felt he was the best person for the job. Ideological passion hampers our ability to work with each other rationally. Compromise is hard, and it is not for the cowardly. When it comes to saving the planet, its people, and the myriad of creatures that share the earth with us, I would rather be a compromiser than a loser.

Most Americans want a healthy economy and environment. To

Contrary to conventional wisdom, states can protect the environment and promote a strong economy. In a 2000 study by the Institute for Southern Studies that ranked all fifty states, seven states scored in the top fifteen for both economic and environmental health. "Top performers" on both the Gold (economic) and Green (environmental) scales were:

Vermont (Gold 3; Green 1)
Minnesota (Gold 2, Green 6)
Rhode Island (Gold 4, Green 4)
Colorado (Gold 5, Green 14)
Maine (Gold 13, Green 7)
Maryland (Gold 6, Green 15)
Wisconsin (Gold 11, Green 12)

Sacrificing environmental protection won't ensure economic prosperity. Many government and business leaders claim that enacting and enforcing strong environmental measures would hurt economic growth in their state. But lax environmental standards have little economic payoff and may hurt long-term economic prospects. Ten states—many in the South—rank in the cellar on both environmental and economic scales:

Louisiana (Gold rank 48, Green rank 50)
Alabama (Gold 47, Green 49)
Texas (Gold 43, Green 46)
Tennessee (Gold 45, Green 46)
Mississippi (Gold 50, Green 38)
Indiana (Gold 40, Green 48)
Arkansas (Gold 49, Green 37)
West Virginia (Gold 46, Green 39)
Kentucky (Gold 44, Green 41)
South Carolina (Gold 38, Green 45)

TEN CONVENIENT TRUTHS OF
CONSERVATION PROGRESS

1). *We have two choices in conservation: genuine bipartisan engagement with each other and compromise, or failure.* Our progress to date exemplifies this principle. Today, there are those on both sides of the environmental issue who would rather fail than engage or compromise.

2). *Environmental conservation is not a conservative or liberal cause—it is everyone's cause.* It is certainly not a counterculture cause, and treating it that way leads to failure by driving people away from an issue they are predisposed to support.

3). *Practically speaking, and functionally in the case of the US Senate, a supermajority is needed to make durable progress on any issue.* Partisan rivals with harsh campaigns can usually stop each other's initiatives, but durable progress requires a strong majority. The prospects for success on any issue are always directly proportional to the broadness of the base of support. Most major steps forward in conservation have been compromises crafted by a diverse group of stakeholders.

4). *Progress comes incrementally.* When incremental progress becomes unacceptable, when the perfect becomes the enemy of the good, it results in a stalemate where progress halts.

5). *Most major national environment progress was made during Republican presidencies in cooperation with Democrats in Congress.* Theodore Roosevelt protected more land than any president in history. Nixon and Ford signed more environmental legislation. Ronald Reagan signed into law twice as many new wilderness areas as any other president and signed the Montreal Protocol in 1988—the most important environmental initiative in human history. Unfortunately, the leadership of today's Republican Party seems to have abandoned this heritage, even while some Democrats have obstructed incremental progress.

6). *A lack of civility in rhetoric and tactics correlates with failure and a lack of conservation progress.* Presenting solutions, expressing concern about lost opportunities, and engaging Americans in "can do" thinking are better ways to generate interest in conservation and make progress. From 1988 to 2012, when opposition to taxes has become a gospel, voters have directly approved $57.5 billion in ballots for local tax increases to fund open-space bonds and other land conservation. If you look at the campaign materials for these initiatives, you see little strident rhetoric and a lot of practical solutions.

7). *Constructive engagement with business may be the most critical factor to conservation success overall.* Paul Hawken, author of *The Ecology of Commerce,* said it best: "Ironically, business contains our blessing. It must, because no other institution in the modern world is powerful enough to foster the necessary changes." There is no doubt that some business practices have been shortsighted, stupid, or even criminal, but business is not a monolith. Conservationists need to engage with thoughtful business leaders.

8). *Individual action cannot be a substitute for collective action.* Leading by example and showing what is possible can be a good thing, but when individual action gives people the sense they are doing something effective and thereby do not need to support societal action, it can be counterproductive.

9). *Radical environmentalism is in outcome effectively anti-environmental.* Any cause that is intimidated and silenced in the face of its extremes becomes defined by them.

10). *To succeed, a new approach to environmental protection is needed that embraces strategic compromise and respectful engagement.* Compromise is not cowardice, and kindness should not be mistaken for weakness.

achieve both, we need a new approach to environmental protection based on mutual civility and respect. Our past success in conservation is based on these Ten Convenient Truths of Conservation Progress.

Asking young people to embrace these truths is asking them to do something very difficult, something that most of my generation has been unable to do. The very idea of bipartisan cooperation seems highly offensive to ideological purists of both the left wing and the right wing. People who truly wish to seek consensus solutions are confronted with the double burden of working out the substantial differences they have with each other, while fending off ideological purists from both sides who insist that any compromise is both unnecessary and unwise.

Conservation success and the greatest political changes in the world have their source in an approach that emphasizes reconciliation, outreach, and compromise. Just look at South Africa and the legacy of Nelson Mandela, where policies of engagement, compromise, and forgiveness are healing a nation from one of the great atrocities of the last century—apartheid. After twenty-seven years of unjust imprisonment, Mandela stuck with his belief in compromise and reconciliation. He did so even as his friends and other members of the African National Congress where being killed or exiled in South Africa. He emphasized that is was a bad system that needed to be removed and had the wisdom to graciously acknowledge the white South Africans who had been essential to the cause of freedom and justice. He left his heart open and reassured white South Africans that they were needed to be part of the country's future. He was able to deliver that message fluently in both English and Afrikaans. In the end, 69 percent of white South Africa voted in favor of the negotiations that led to an end to apartheid and to the free elections that made Nelson Mandela president of South Africa.

If the next generation of conservation leaders can find a way to reach out for success on such a consensus popular issue as conservation, just maybe they can show the way to shake off the partisan paralysis that threatens our nation and our future in so many other ways. If they can succeed where we have not, it will be because they have realized that compromise is essential to the function of a democracy and to the success of the great democratic tradition that is the protection of the natural heritage of our homeland.

Additional Reading

While most of this book is based on the author's personal experiences, readers may find these titles to be of interest.

Anderson, Ray, with Robin White. *Confessions of a Radical Industrialist: Profits, People, Purpose—Doing Business by Respecting the Earth.* New York: St. Martin's Press, 2009.

Collins, Jim. *Good to Great and the Social Sectors: Why Business Thinking Is Not the Answer.* Monograph. Boulder, Colo.: Jim Collins, 2005.

Diamond, Jared. *Collapse: How Societies Choose to Fail or Succeed.* New York: Penguin Books, 2005.

Duda, Mark Damian; Martin F. Jones; and Andrea Criscione. *The Sportsman's Voice: Hunting and Fishing in America.* State College, Penn.: Venture Publishing, 2010.

Eiseley, Loren. *The Immense Journey: An Imaginative Naturalist Explores the Mysteries of Man and Nature.* New York: Random House, 1946.

Hacker, Jacob S., and Paul Pierson. *Winner-Take-All Politics.* New York: Simon & Schuster, 2010.

Halstead, Ted, and Michael Lind. *The Radical Center: The Future of American Politics.* New York: Doubleday, 2001.

Hawken, Paul. *The Ecology of Commerce: A Declaration of Sustainability.* New York: Harper Business, 1993.

Hesselbein, Francis; Marshall Goldsmith; and Richard Beckhard, eds. *The Leader of the Future: New Visions, Strategies, and Practices for the Next Era.* San Francisco: Jossey-Bass, 1996.

Jones, Van, with Ariane Conrad. *The Green Collar Economy: How One Solution Can Fix Our Two Biggest Problems.* New York: HarperOne, 2008.

Kromm, Chris; Keith Ernst; and Jaffer Battica. *Gold and Green 2000.* Durham, NC. Institute for Southern Studies. 2000. Available at http://www.southernstudies.org/southern_exposure/2000/11/report-gold-and-green-2000.html as *Report Gold and Green.*

Leopold, Aldo. *A Sand County Almanac.* New York: Oxford University Press, 1949.

Luntz, Frank. *Words That Work: It's Not What You Say, It's What People Hear.* New York: Hyperion Books, 2007.

Mandela, Nelson Rolihlahla. *Long Walk to Freedom: The Autobiography of Nelson Mandela.* New York: Little Brown, 1994.

Matthiessen, Peter, drawings by Bob Hines. *Wildlife in America.* New York: Viking, 1959.

Myers, Norman, and Jennifer Kent. *Perverse Subsidies: How Tax Dollars Can Undercut the Environment and the Economy.* Washington, DC: Island Press, 2001.

Orr, David. *Earth in Mind: On Education, Environment, and the Human Prospect.* Washington, DC: Island Press, 1994.

Peterson, Peter G. *Running on Empty: How the Democrat and Republican Parties Are Bankrupting Our Future and What Americans Can Do about It.* New York: Farrar, Straus and Giroux, 2004.

Russell, Terry, and Renny Russell. *On the Loose.* San Francisco: Sierra Club, 1967.

Safina, Carl. *Song for the Blue Ocean: Encounters along the World's Coasts and beneath the Seas.* New York: Henry Holt, 1997.

Schlesinger, Joe. *Time Zones: A Journalist in the World.* Toronto: Random House, 1990.

Wilson, Edward O. *The Future of Life.* New York: Random House, 2002.

Index

Abbey, Edward, 43, 45, 133
abortion, 20, 44–45, 44
Acadia National Parks, 77
acid rain, xiv, 9, 18, 27, 30–32, 34, 143
Adirondack Mountains, 31
adversarial advocacy; effectiveness of, 2
African National Congress, 160
AIDS; population control and, 45
Alaska Lands Act, 9
American Forest and Paper Association, 60, 72, 140
American Wildlife Conservation Partners, 9, 83–84
America's Voice for Conservation, Recreation, and Preservation, 98
An Inconvenient Truth, 121–122
Antioch College; Vietnam War protest and, 6

Antiquities Act of 1906, 76–77
Arctic National Wildlife Refuge, 126
Aspinall, Wayne, 134
Association of Fish and Wildlife Agencies, 96
Association of State Dam Safety Officials, 131

Babbit, Bruce, 128
Bartholomew I; 2002 Proclamation in Optimism and, 27; environmental policy and, 47
Bass Pro Shops, 95
Battelle Pacific Northwest National Laboratory; InEnTec LLC's Plasma Enhanced Melter and, 39
Beringia South; ravens and elevated blood levels of iron, 91

Blank, Arthur, 71–72
Boise Cascade forest products company, 142
Boone and Crockett Club, 83
Boschwitz, Rudy, 143
Boundary Waters Canoe Area Wilderness (BWCAW), 112–113
Bowles, Erskine, 139
Bradley, Russ, 6
Brooks, David; all or nothing phenomenon and, 126–127; on activism and, 15
Brower, David, 132
BTUs; solid waste production and, 39
Budget Control Act of 2011, 136
Bureau of Land Management, 61, 64
Burns, Ken, 95
Bush, George H. W., 18; acid rain and, 30–31; air pollution breakthroughs and, 153; Antiquities Act and, 77; Clean Air Act (1990) and, 124
Bush, George W., 18; 1984 Mexico City policy and, 45; 2000 election and, 122; Antiquities Act and, 77; Christie Todd Whitman and, 123; Clean Air Interstate Rule and, 34; investment in clean air and, 33; Pacific Remote Islands National Monument and, 77; Papahanaumokuakea Marine National Monument and, 77; population of grizzly bears and, 143; roadless rule and, 66–71
business conservation; "adversary ambassadors" and, 58; environmental sustainability and shareholder value, 52; overview of, 51–52; proximity reduces prejudice and, 53; real long-term wealth and, 56–57

Cabela's; outdoor gear store and, 95
California Energy Commission, 36
Canadian Broadcasting Corporation, 11
Canadian Coalition on Acid Rain, 31
Canyonlands National Park, 129

Census Bureau; Americans in extreme poverty and, 138
Centennial Forest Congress, 73
Center for Biological Diversity, 82, 90
Chaffee, John; acid rain and, 30
Cheney, Dick, 124
Chicago Cubs; Herb Smith and, 50
chlorofluorocarbons (CFCs); economic profit from, 27; Montreal Protocol of Substances that Deplete the Ozone Layer and, 29; ozone layer and, 28; profits from, 28; reduction of, 29
Churchill, Winston, 128
Chu, Steven, 107
CIA; national security benefits of energy efficiency and, 38
Citizen Management Committee; population of grizzly bears and, 143
Clean Air Act (1990), 18, 31–34, 124, 143
Clean Air Act of 1970, 16–18
Clean Air Interstate Rule; pollution reduction and, 34
Clean Water Act (1972), 17–18
climate change; chlorofluorocarbons (CFCs) and, 29; Copenhagen Summit (2009), 18–19, 35; Kyoto Protocol (1997), 19, 35; lack of progress on, 17; Montreal Protocol of Substances that Deplete the Ozone and, 34; overview of, 35–36; Rio de Janeiro Earth Summit (1992), 19, 35
Clinton, Bill, 122; 1984 Mexico City policy and, 45; 2000 Roadless Rule and, 62–67, 69; Antiquities Act and, 77; arsenic in drinking water and, 123–124
Coalition for Ducks, Wetlands, and Clean Water, 105
Coalition on the Environment and Jewish Life; environmental policy and, 46
Collapse: How Societies Choose to Fail or Succeed (Diamond), 23, 50, 60
Colorado River, 129, 132

Comprehensive Environmental Response, Compensation and Liability Act (Superfund), 16
Concord Coalition, 136, 139
Conoco Philips, 54–55
conservation; as best business practice and, 24; as righteous issue and, 15–16; collaboration and, 140–146; diversity of interests and, 6; double hulls for hazardous cargo and, 110–111; "healthy forests" and, 67–68; history of misunderstanding and, 78–83; land conservation and, 114–120; "Minnesota nice" and, 22; progress and, 3; spending and national debt, 135–139; ten convenient truths of conservation success and, 152–160; waste-to-energy projects and, 39
Conservation and Reinvestment Act (CARA), 117–119
Conservation Fund, 55, 72, 96, 114
conservation groups; history of, 76–77
Conservation International, 114
contraception, 20, 44–45
Coolidge, Calvin, 27
Cooperative Alliance for Refuge Enhancement (CARE); allies of, 97–98
Copenhagen Summit (2009); climate change and, 18–19, 35
Corporate Average Fuel Economy (CAFE); efficiency of America's automobile fleet and, 37
Cosco, Jon M., 132
Costs and Benefits of Regulation; investment in clean air and, 33
Craig, Robert, 144
Curecanti Dam, 132

Darling, Stan; acid rain and, 31
DDT pesticide; Tom DeLay and, 29
Deepwater Horizon, 21, 155
Defenders of Wildlife, 81, 97
DeLay, Tom; repealing CFC ban and, 29
Devil's Tower, 77

Diamond, Jared; conservation of business and, 50; constructive engagement with business and, 23; deforestation and, 60
Dingell-Johnson Act, 93
Dinosaur National Monument, 129–130, 132–134
Dionne, E. J., 114
Dodd, Chris; broken political system and, 5
Dombeck, Mike, 65, 70
Doolittle, John; repealing CFC ban and, 29
double hulls; hazardous cargo and, 110–111
Douglas, Marjory Stoneman, 147
Dow Corning; processing industrial waste and, 40
Drucker, Peter, 5, 58, 152
Ducks Unlimited, 76, 83, 94, 96
DuPont; CFC production and, 29; cost-effective energy reduction and, 19; William K. Reilly and, 55
Durenberger, David; acid rain and, 30

Earth Day 1970, 76; garbage production and, 151
Earth Day 2005; "Vote Yes for Water Quality" campaign and, 105
Earth in the Balance (Gore), 122
Earthjustice, 66, 81
Echo Park, 129, 133–134
Echo Park Dam, 131–132
Echo Park, Struggle for Preservation (Cosco), 132
Ecology of Commerce (Hawken), 23, 50, 159
Einstein, Albert; quote on insanity and, 1
Eiseley, Loren; The Immense Journey and, 1
Eisenhower, Dwight D., 132
Endangered Species Act, 16–17, 93–94, 143

Enerkem; solid waste-to-biofuels production facility and, 40
environmental awareness; increase in, 6;
land protection ballot measures and,
116; sea-level rise and, 8
Environmental Defense, 81
Environmental Defense Fund; "cap and
trade" approach and, 32
environmentalists; infighting and, 121–
123; Nader nadir and, 121–127; nuclear
waste and, 107; perils of compromise
and, 128–134; reaching outside our
groups to others and, 15
environmental protection; activist approach and, 13; double hulls for hazardous cargo and, 110–111; progress
of, 2; ten convenient truths of conservation success and, 152–160
Environmental Protection Agency
(EPA), 16, 123–124; Doug Smith and,
51; environmental success of 1990
Clean Air Act and, 34; investment in
clean air and, 33; lead bullets and,
90–91; raw sewage in waterways and,
17; Southern Company lawsuit
and, 34
Escalante Grand Staircase National
Monument, 77
ethanol, 37, 39–40, 49
Ethanol Boosting System, 37
Evangelical Environmental Network;
environmental policy and, 46, 48
Exxon *Valdez*, 20, 110

Fairbank, Maslin, Maullin, Metz &
Associates; bipartisan research team
and, 75; funding for conservation and,
137–138
Federal Advisory Committee Act of
1972, 16, 68
Federal Land Management and Policy
Act of 1976, 16
Federal Water Pollution Control Act of
1972, 16

Ferris, Don, 125
fishing; Bass Pro Shops and, 95; Fish
and Wildlife restoration funding and,
93; statistics for, 78
Flaming Gorge Dam, 132
Ford, Gerald, 12, 16, 153, 158
Ford, Henry, 140
Foreign Assistance Act; abortion and, 45
Forest and Rangeland Renewable Resources Planning Act of 1974, 16
forest certification, 71–74
Forest Congresses, 73
forest products businesses; "healthy
forests" and, 67–68; impact of clear-
cuts to water quality and wildlife, 61;
overview of, 60–61; roadless rule and,
62–67; Wilderness Act and, 63
Forest Resource Act of 1894, 76
forestry practices; inventoried roadless
areas (IRA) and, 64; restoration
and, 62
Forest Stewardship Council, 71, 73
Franklin, Benjamin, 75
Fraser, John; acid rain and, 31–32
Friedman, Tom, 139
Friends of the Boundary Waters Wilderness, 112–113
Friends of the Earth, 81
Fuller, Kathryn S., 55
Function 300, 137; spending on conser-
vation and natural resources, 151
Furtman, Mike, 141–142

Glacier National Park, 130, 133
Glen Canyon, 129, 134
Glen Canyon Dam, 132–133
Glen Canyon Institute, 133
Global Biodiversity Outlook (2010),
147–150
Gold and Green 2000; state's economic
and environmental performance, 155
Gore, Al, 67, 122; 2000 election and,
122; *An Inconvenient Truth*, 122; *Earth
in the Balance* and, 122

Governor's Conference on Natural Resources, 77
Graham, John B.; investment in clean air and, 33
Grand Canyon, 77, 133
Grand Canyon National Park, 133
Grand Teton National Park, 100–101
Grant, Bud, 105
Greater Yellowstone Coalition, 66, 70
Green Group, 9; business conservation and, 56; forum of CEOs and, 79; hunters and, 88; list of member organizations and, 80; major national environmental group CEOs and, 55; Sundance resort and, 85
greenhouse gas emissions; converting municipal garbage into fuel and, 40
Green like God (Merritt), 48
Greenpeace, 81; nuclear energy and, 109
Green River, 129–130, 132
Gulf of Mexico; oil spills and, 21
Gunnison River, 132

Hansen, James, 150
Harvey, Harold; acid rain and, 30
Hawaiian Islands National Wildlife Refuge, 77
Hawken, Paul, 159; conservation of business and, 50; constructive engagement with business and, 23
Hawkins, David, 15
Hayes, Denis; founder of Earth Day and, 51
Healthy Forest Restoration Act, 68
Heissenbuttel, John, 60
Heston, Charlton; population control and, 45; population growth and, 43
Historic Preservation Fund, 118
HIV AIDS; population control and, 45
Home Depot, 72
hunting; assault rifles and, 89; Fish and Wildlife restoration funding and, 93; lead bullets and, 90–92; poaching epi-

demic in Louisiana and, 104; statistics for, 78; understanding hunters and, 85–89
Hurley, Adele; acid rain and, xiv, 31

Idaho Conservation League, 70
InEnTec LLC's; Plasma Enhanced Melter and, 39
Institute for Southern Studies; state's economic and environmental performance, 155; study results and, 157
Intergovernmental Panel on Climate Change, 150
International Energy Agency; carbon dioxide emissions and, 35–36; OPEC revenue and, 41
International Paper, 55; Mark Suwyn and, 51
inventoried roadless areas (IRA), 64
Izaak Walton League of America, x, 9, 50, 53, 56, 58, 62, 66, 76, 81–83, 87, 94, 109, 112, 125–126, 131–132, 134
Izaak Walton League v. Agriculture Secretary Earl Butz, 62

Janik, Phil, 72
John Paul II; 2002 Proclamation in Optimism and, 27; environmental policy and, 47
Johnson, Lyndon, 12
Jones, Van, 156

Keillor, Garrison, 103, 106
Keystone Center, 94, 144–145
King, Colbert I.; ideological and partisan rivals, 11
Kings Canyon National Park, 130
Koppel, Ted, 154
Kyoto Protocol (1997); climate change and, 19, 35

Lacey Act of 1900, 76
Lake Erie, 85
Lake Pepin, 109–110

Land and Water Conservation Fund,
118–119, 137
land conservation; acres covered and, 115;
Conservation and Reinvestment Act
(CARA), 117–119; Land and Water
Conservation Fund (LWCF) and,
118–119, 137; land protection ballot
measures and, 116; Land Trust Al-
liance and, 81, 114–115; overview of,
114–115
Land Trust Alliance, 81, 114–115
land trusts; open space and habitat con-
servation, 22
LandVote; tax increases for land conser-
vation initiatives and, 115
Lawrence Berkeley National Lab, 36
League of Conservation Voters, 81,
143–144
Leopold, Aldo, 75, 81, 103, 121, 140,
146, 152
Lessard, Bob, 104
LL Bean; outdoor gear store and, 95
Lodore Canyon, 129–130, 133
Louisiana-Pacific, 50–52, 55–57, 126

Mahoney, Shane, 89
Mammoth Cave National Park, 130
Mandela, Nelson, 121, 160
Marine Mammal Protection Act of
1972, 16
Massachusetts Institute of Technology;
ethanol and, 37; InEnTec LLC's
Plasma Enhanced Melter and, 39
McConnell, Mitch; broken political
system and, 5
McKinsey and Company; environmental
sustainability and shareholder value,
52; improving energy efficiency and,
36; reducing concentrations of carbon
dioxide and, 19
Mdewakanton Sioux, 107
Merlo, Harry, 50–51
Merritt, Jonathan; environmental policy
and, 48

military overflights, 112–113
Miller, George, 118
Minneapolis Star Tribune; decline in
Minnesota hunting, fishing, and water
quality, 104
Minnesota; conservation funding mea-
sure and, 103–104; Institute for South-
ern Studies and, 157; "Minnesota nice"
and, 22; nuclear waste storage and,
107–108; pumped storage power and,
109–110; "Vote Yes for Water Quality"
campaign and, 105
Minnesota Department of Health; lead
bullets and, 90–91
Minnesota Game and Fish study; lead
bullets and, 91
Minnesota Public Utility Board, 108
Minnesota Vikings, 105
Mississippi River, 107, 109–110
Molina, Mario, chlorofluorocarbons
(CFCs) and, 28
Moment of Truth report, 139
Monongahela National Forest and; law-
suit on, 62
Montreal Protocol, 158
Montreal Protocol of Substances that
Deplete the Ozone; climate change
and, 34; production of CFCs
and, 29
Moore, Henson, 72
Muir, John, 131
Mule Deer Foundation, 83
Mullen, Mike; environmental strategy
and, 7
Mulroney, Brian; acid rain and, 30, 31;
John Fraser and, 32
Murie, Margaret, 102

Nader, Ralph, 2000 election and, 122
National Academy of Sciences; arsenic
in drinking water and, 123
National Audubon Society, 76, 81, 97
National Council of Churches of Christ;
environmental policy and, 46

national debt; Americans in extreme poverty and, 138; Budget Control Act of 2011 and, 136; environmental spending and, 135–139; Moment of Truth report, 139

National Environmental Policy Act of 1970, 16–17

National Environmental Scorecard; League of Conservation Voters, 143–144

National Forest Management Act of 1976, 16, 62

National Parks Conservation Association, 131

National Park Service, 61, 63, 98, 133

National Religious Partnership on the Environment; environmental policy and, 46

National Resources Defense Council, 15

National Rifle Association, 89, 97

National Wilderness Preservation System, 63–64

National Wildlife Federation, 82

National Wildlife Foundation, 81

National Wildlife Refuge System, 97–98

National Wild Turkey Federation, 83

Natural Resources Defense Council, 66, 81, 123

Nature Conservancy, 9, 55, 66, 80–81, 96, 114–115

Navajo Dam, 132

New York Times; David Brooks on activism and, 15

Nigeria; oil spills and, 20

Nixon, Richard, 12, 16, 77, 153, 158

Nokes, Jim, xv, 54

Noonan, Pat, xiii, 51, 55, 72

North American Wetland Conservation Act, 137

North American Wildlife and Natural Resources Conference, 83

North Dakota Department of Health; lead bullets and, 90–91

Northern States Power, 107–108

Obama, Barack, 18, 22; 1984 Mexico City policy and, 45; efficiency of America's automobile fleet and, 37; Tom Vilsack and, 70

Oberlin College, 149

Office of Management and Budget, investment in clean air and, 18, 33

oil development; imported oil and, 20

O'Keefe, Georgia, 133

OPEC; oil consumption and, 38; revenue and, 41

Oregon Nature Conservancy, 52

Orr, David, 149

Outdoor America; Izaak Walton League of America and, 126

Outdoor Life; Jim Zumbo and, 89

Outdoor Writers Association of America (OWAA); Sierra Club and, 89

ozone hole, 27–29

Pachauri, Rajendra, 150

Pacific Remote Islands National Monument, 77

Papahanaumokuakea Marine National Monument, 77

Partnership Project; web site for, 79

Pawlenty, Tim, 104

Peabody Energy Company, 55

Penfold, Joe, 132, 134

Perley, Michael; acid rain and, xiv, 31

Peterson, Max, 72

Pew Center for Climate Change, 82, 99

Pfeiffer, Martin, 31; "biostitutes" and, 30

Pheasants Forever, 83, 94, 96

Pinchot, Gifford, 131

Pittman-Robertson Act, 93

politics; approval rating for Congress and, 154; broken political system and, 5; "Contract with America" and, 21; environmental progress in 1970s and, 21; environmental votes in congress and, 17–18; environment as campaign issue and, 12; "gotcha" politics and, 153; land protection ballot measures and,

politics (*continued*)
116; nuclear waste and, 107; pragmatism over partisanship and, 4; Vietnam War and, 6–7
polling; conservation and, 11, 54, 75; environmental crisis and, 5; environmentalists and, 8; funding for conservation and, 137–138; land conservation initiatives and, 23, 117
population control; gridlock on issue of, 20; overview of, 42–45
Porter, Eliot, 133
Powell, John Wesley, 129
President's Commission on Fiscal Responsibility and Reform, 135
Price Anderson Act, 108
Public Opinion Strategies; bipartisan research team and, 75; funding for conservation and, 137–138

Quail Unlimited, 83
Quakers; Vietnam War protest and, 6

radical environmentalism; anti-environmental in outcome and, 6; as part of the problem and, 2
Reagan, Ronald, 17; 1984 Mexico City policy and, 45; acid rain and, 30–31; air pollution breakthroughs and, 153; Antiquities Act and, 77; Montreal Protocol and, 158; Wilderness Act and, 63
Redford, Robert, 85
REI; outdoor gear store and, 95
Reilly, William K., 31, 55
religion; environmental policy and, 46–49
Resource Conservation and Recovery Act, 16
Rio de Janeiro Earth Summit (1992); climate change and, 35; climate change pollutants and, 19; United Nation's Conference on Environment and Development, 71

Risch, Jim; 2000 Roadless Rule and, 69–70
Roadless Area Conservation National Advisory Committee; roadless forestland and, 68–69
Rocky Mountain Elk Foundation, 83, 94, 96
Roosevelt, Franklin, 130
Roosevelt, IV, Theodore, 99, 101–102, 142
Roosevelt, Theodore, 12, 57, 76–78, 99, 117, 153
Rosenfeld, Art; energy efficiency expert and, 36
Rowland, Sherwood; chlorofluorocarbons (CFCs) and, 28
Ruffed Grouse Society, 83

Safari Club International, 97, 102
Safe Water Drinking Act, 123
Sand County Almanac (Leopold), 75, 81, 146, 152
San Juan River, 132
Schlesinger, Joe; signs of madness and, 11
Schweitzer, Albert, 114
sea-level rise; big global issue and, 8
Securities Exchange Commission, 73
Selway-Salmon-Bitterroot Ecosystem, 142
Seventh Forest Congress, 71, 73
Shark Finning Prohibition Act of 2000, 143–144
Sierra Club, 36, 66, 76, 81–82, 88–89, 131–133
Sikorski, Gerry; acid rain and, 30
Simpson, Alan, 135, 139
Smith, Doug; EPA inspector and, 51
Smith, Herb; Izaak Walton League of America and, 50
Smith, Robert Angus; acid rain and, 30
Society of American Foresters, 72
solar energy, 42
Southern Company; lawsuit and clean air rule, 34

Southern Minnesota Municipal Power
    Agency (SMMPA), 109–110
Sowald, Don, 113
Sparrowe, Rollin, 97
Split Mountain Canyon, 129–130, 133
Stafford, Robert; acid rain and, 30
St. Lawrence River, 150
sulfur dioxide; concentrations of, 34
Sustainable Forestry Initiative, 71–73;
    7th Forest Congress and, 51
Suwyn, Mark, xiv, 51–52

Ten Convenient Truths of Conservation
    Progress, 152–160
Theodore Roosevelt Conservation
    Alliance, 83
Theodore Roosevelt Conservation
    Partnership, 66, 70
Thomas, Jack Ward, 64–65, 70, 72
timber harvests; in national forests
    and, 20
Toxic Substance Control Act of
    1976, 16
Trojan nuclear plant, 108
Trout Unlimited, 66, 70, 83, 94, 99
Trust for Public Land, 96, 114
Turner, John F., xiii, 55
Twain, Mark, 102, 111

Uinta Mountains, 129
United Nation's Conference on Environ-
    ment and Development; Rio Earth
    Summit and, 71
United Nations Environment Program;
    financial system collapse and, 25
United States; dam-building era in, 131;
    fishing and, 78; forestry in, 61–62;
    hunting and, 78; solid waste produc-
    tion and, 39; Treasury Department's
    2011 Financial Report and, 136; yearly
    use of gasoline and diesel fuel, 41
University of Minnesota–Duluth, 106
Upper Mississippi Wildlife and Fish
    Refuges, 111

Urban Park and Recreation Recovery
    program, 118
US Bureau of Reclamation; five major
    dam projects and, 130
US Conference of Catholic Bishops;
    environmental policy and, 46
US Departments of Interior and Com-
    merce; wildlife-dependent recreation
    and, 93
US Fish and Wildlife Refuges, 64
US Fish and Wildlife Service, 55, 61,
    142; lead bullets and, 91; poaching
    epidemic in Louisiana and, 104
US Forest Service, 61, 63–64, 66–67,
    70, 72–73, 112, 131
US Supreme Court; Clinton roadless
    rule and, 70–71

Vietnam War; protest and, 6
Vilsack, Tom, 70
Vogt, Bill, 132

Wallop-Breaux amendment; fuel taxes
    and, 93
Wall Street Journal; white roofs
    and, 36
Washington Post; ideological and par-
    tisan rivals, 11
Waste Management; solid waste-to-
    biofuels production facility and, 40
Waterman, Julie, xv, 79
Waxman, Henry; acid rain and, 30
Whitetails Unlimited, 83
Whitman, Christie Todd, 123–124
Wilderness Act of 1964, 17, 63–64
Wilderness Society, 99
Wildlife Management Institute, 66,
    76, 83, 97, 131
Wildlife Society, 90
Wildlife Urban Interface, 68
Wilson, Edward O., 147
Wilson, Woodrow, 129–130
wind energy, 42
Wind River Range, 129

Woolsey, Jim; national security benefits
    of energy efficiency and, 38
World Energy Outlook 2012; carbon diox-
    ide emissions and, 35–36
World Resources Institute, 81, 99
World Wildlife Fund, 55, 81
Wright Patterson Air Force Base, 6

Yampa River, 130, 133
Yellowstone National Park, 22, 96, 99–101

Yellowstone Park Foundation, 54
Young, Don, 118
Yucca Mountain, 107

Zentner, Dave, xiv, 106
Zumbo, Jim; assault rifles and, 89

OTHER TITLES IN THE
CONSERVATION LEADERSHIP SERIES:

Money for the Cause: A Complete Guide to Event Fundraising
Rudolph A. Rosen

On Politics and Parks
George L. Bristol

Hillingdon Ranch: Four Seasons, Six Generations
David K. Langford and Lorie Woodward Cantu